Liguria

THE COOKBOOK

Liguria

THE COOKBOOK

Recipes from the Italian Riviera
Laurel Evans

Photographs by Emilio Scoti

RIZZOLI
NEW YORK

New York · Paris · London · Milan

La Mia Liguria

The first time I set my eyes on my future mother-in-law, she was tiptoeing her way down a narrow, twisting road (a road I would eventually come to know so well), sporting a breezy white linen dress, bright red lipstick, and an enviable tan. She squeezed my hand and smiled widely as I clumsily spat out a much-practiced, yet poorly executed Italian greeting. After an animated and incomprehensible exchange of foreign words with her son, my boyfriend Emilio, she trotted off to the market as we continued up the hillside amidst wild blackberry bushes and fig trees until rounding a bend and stopping in front of a creaking, green iron gate. The house, a three-story, thick-walled villa nestled between olive trees and rose bushes, looked over the small, colorful village of Moneglia. Just beyond, the turquoise expanse of the Mediterranean sprawled lazily towards the horizon. I ran my fingers through my hair and smoothed my shirt. My bright red faux hawk, cut-off military pants, and vintage T-shirt were suddenly feeling less than appropriate. I grabbed Emilio's hand and stepped boldly through the gate.

Liguria, the Italian Riviera, is the stuff of postcards and novels. This crescent shaped slice of heaven stretches over two hundred miles of coastline from France to Tuscany. Steep green hills plunge dramatically into the deep blue sea, pastel houses perch impossibly on cliffsides, fuchsia bougainvillea cascades off balconies, secret, overgrown gardens and ornate iron gates conceal baroque mansions of a bygone era of grandeur. Sunny beaches are lined with colorful, striped umbrellas and carpeted with glistening sunbathers. Winding roads lead to the sea, framed by oleander and palm trees, twisting through olive groves and orange trees. It's no surprise that writers, poets, and artists have been flocking to the water's edge here for centuries: D.H. Lawrence, Ernest Hemingway, Ezra Pound, Lord Byron, and

Mary Shelley were all regulars of these small, multicolored seaside villages. But, while these picturesque, well-traveled tourist routes do live up to their hype, there is much more to Liguria.

This is a land of contradictions, defined both by the extravagance of wealthy, baroque, cosmopolitan Genoa, and by the thrift and ingenuity of the hard-pressed, arduous *entroterra* (inlands). Genoa, once a powerful maritime republic, was an important center of commerce and trade throughout the Middle Ages and Renaissance, infusing the region not only with economic power, but also with exotic flavors from the world over. Genoa is the epicenter of Liguria, both sentimentally and geographically. Locals refer to everything east of Genoa as the *Riviera di Levante*, and everything west of the city as the *Riviera di Ponente*, or simply refer to the two areas as *Levante* (which means "where the sun rises") and *Ponente* (where the sun sets).

Liguria is surrounded by some of the best eating destinations on the planet: France to the west, Piedmont to the north, Emilia-Romagna to the east, and Tuscany to the south. Italian cuisine, in all its manifestations and all over the world, never goes out of style. Yet Liguria, except for focaccia and pesto, has been

Vintage postcard from
Moneglia, 1914

largely overlooked from a culinary standpoint. This region offers a treasure trove of recipes that are inventive, seasonal, waste-conscious, and often plant-forward. Because it was a poor cuisine, meat was used sparingly, and vegetables were often cleverly transformed into various main dishes, with the skillful use of a few key flavor enhancers like salt-packed anchovies, pine nuts, dried mushrooms, and aged cheeses. Many of these recipes are based on economy and thrift, and ingeniously recycle ingredients and leftovers into various new dishes. The pleasant Mediterranean climate produces some of the most flavorful herbs, fruits, and vegetables I've ever tasted, which Ligurians deftly transform into hearty and flavorful meals.

Which brings us back to my first dinner in Moneglia, a small, charming village in the *Riviera di Levante*. This was my big debut, my first introduction to the family. Emilio was working in Texas at the time and we had met in my small hometown. I was twenty years old, curious, lost, and hungry for life. Though we had only been dating for three weeks, Emilio had already told his family a lot about his tall Texan girlfriend, and expectations were high. That night, fifteen adults and a handful of children settled around the long marble table under the large pine tree in the front yard, overlooking the darkening sea as dusk fell upon the hillside. Inside, three tiny, powerful, and chatty *nonne* bustled about the crowded kitchen, shouting orders while putting finishing touches on the evening's meal. A parade of culinary delights followed: fried zucchini blossoms, savory vegetable tarts, homemade pesto with fresh pasta and green beans, braised rabbit with pine nuts and olives, all accompanied by a river of local vermentino and exuberant conversation. The meal lasted for hours. I couldn't remember ever spending that much time around a table, and I loved every minute. Accustomed to the efficient, often perfunctory style of many American meals, this lively feast was a revelation to me. By the third course I had long forgotten my inappropriate attire, and by the third glass of wine I was feeling improbably fluent in Italian.

"I can live with this," I thought as I tossed back another glass and accepted second helpings of everything.

And live with it I did: Over the following fifteen years, Moneglia became my summer sanctuary and my winter refuge. We settled in the bustling, lively city of Milan where Emilio pursued his photography and I finished my degree at design school. As the months stretched into years, I began writing cookbooks and blogging in Italian about American cuisine, every new recipe dutifully photographed by Emilio. Food became the bridge between my old life and my new one; it helped mitigate my homesickness and assimilate me into a new culture. Though we lived and worked two hours away in the big city, we spent our summers, and almost every weekend, in our tiny seaside town. Instead of passing all my days at the beach, I puttered around the kitchen with three lively *nonne*, basking in the smells and sounds of their expert craft, asking questions in broken Italian, and scribbling recipes in a battered journal. These three women were my gateway into the world of Italian cuisine, and more specifically to the recipes of Liguria. I didn't know at the time, but that boyfriend was my future husband, the father of my children, and that journal was the beginning of this book.

This is my ode to Liguria, a celebration of the region that has captured the hearts and minds of poets and tourists for centuries, but has also become my second home. It is a mere taste, a first glimpse of the vastly complicated and multifaceted Italian Riviera that deserves lifetimes to fully discover. This book is the deeply personal result of my gastronomic adventures over the years: portraits of the locals I have encountered, the landscapes I have relished, the food I've eaten, and the recipes I've recreated along the way. From traditional basil pesto inspired by those three dynamic grandmothers in a hillside villa, to the natural wines of a younger generation of heroic winemakers, reclaiming abandoned lands and creating new traditions, I'm excited for you to join me on this delicious journey into the heart of the timeless, yet ever-evolving Liguria.

Above Left: Lidia, Margherita,
and Fernanda, Moneglia, 1947
Above: *Le nonne*, Moneglia, 1982
Left: *Le nonne*, Moneglia, 2019

Le Nonne

The Grandmothers

No one has influenced and inspired my Italian cooking adventures more than my mother-in-law and her two sisters: the *nonne* of our family. They are all steeped in the same tradition and grew up deeply Ligurian, spending the school year in downtown Genoa and summers running wild in Moneglia. Yet, they each have a unique cooking style as distinct as their personalities. I have had the great privilege of getting to know all three of them quite well, as we have spent countless long summer days together in Moneglia. My husband and his cousins refer to them as *le mamme*, the mothers, and our children call them *le nonne*, the grandmothers. They are often referred to indistinctly as a unit: "*Le nonne* called us for dinner," or "*Le nonne* don't want us to play in the living room because they just polished the floors." To complicate matters further I call them all *zia*, Italian for aunt, followed by their family nickname.

Zia Marghe, short for Margherita, the matriarch of the family, always sits at the head of our long summertime table. My husband remembers her as the strictest of the three when he was a child, to be feared and obeyed, but she has grown into a playful and sweet grandmother who works tirelessly to put endless, glorious dishes on the table. She wakes up before the sun and likes to get all the cooking finished early. It's not uncommon for me to fumble into the kitchen for my first coffee of the day and to find Zia Marghe busily cooking in her bathrobe surrounded by onions frying, rabbit stewing, and pasta sauces bubbling. Of the three *nonne*, I think she's the one who loves cooking the most. Her meals are both elaborate and efficient, a mix of practicality and indulgence. I spend many mornings in the kitchen with Zia Marghe, chopping vegetables while sipping coffee, swapping recipes and family gossip. By nine in the morning she has often finished cooking both lunch and dinner for twenty people. Try her *Risotto con erbe aromatiche e olive* on page 94 and *Acciughe ripiene* on page 107.

Zia Naná, or Fernanda, is my mother-in-law, and while she is an excellent cook, she does it more out of duty than passion. If it were up to her, she would fill her days with landscaping and raking leaves. While she doesn't love to cook, she has many delicious recipes up her sleeve. Widowed when her children were very young, Fernanda grew into a tough-as-nails, working, single mom who learned to put healthy, hearty, delicious meals on the table in the least amount of time possible. She's especially deft at seafood or vegetable pasta sauces. While her cooking style is straightforward and utilitarian, she has a well-tuned palate for seasonings and balances her dishes expertly. You'll find her *Torta Pasqualina* recipe on page 157.

Zia Lidia, the youngest sister, is quirky and creative, and has lived in Milan for the last forty years which has expanded both her worldview and cooking style. She is the adventurous, artistic, avant-garde sister, both in the kitchen and in life. She knits, paints, writes poetry, collects ceramics, designs vases, and sews intricate costumes for my children. Zia Lidia constantly experiments with new recipes yet does not shun tradition. A pesto expert, she is the only one I've seen actually make the famous green sauce with the customary mortar and pestle. Zia Lidia is also the dessert-lover of the family and the biggest fan of my brownies. And she is a deft fryer and allowed me to peek over her shoulder for the *Salvia Fritta* recipe on page 30. She also was the first to show me how to make *Pesto Tradizionale* on page 66.

I don't know who I would be, as a person or a cook, without the influence of these three powerful women. Their wisdom, their words, and their recipes weave through my life and surface frequently in this book.

EMILIA ROMAGNA

TUSCANY

GENOA

RECCO

PORTOFINO

MONEGLIA

5 TERRE

LA SPEZIA

LIGURIA

La Vostra Dispensa Ligure

Your Ligurian Pantry

The recipes in this book are organized into courses, like a traditional Italian meal, starting from *Antipasti* (Appetizers), followed by *Primi* (First Courses) which include pasta, rice, and soups. Second courses are split into two chapters: *Pesce* (Fish) and *Carne* (Meat). Vegetables, which are of primary importance in Liguria, earn their own chapter, *Verdure;* many of these recipes can be served as main courses or sides. Focaccias and flatbreads make up the *Forno* (Breads) chapter. Finish up with something sweet in the *Dolci* chapter, and don't forget to pair the whole meal with Ligurian wines, which you'll find in the final chapter, *I Vini della Liguria.*

Ligurian cuisine is based on garden herbs and vegetables, so seek out the freshest, in-season produce possible for each recipe. Want to try *Condiggiòn* (page 38)? Wait until summer, as there is no use wasting your time on mealy, off-season tomatoes. Trust a knowledgeable fishmonger with your seafood, and make sure they are from sustainable sources. Meat, while rarely the centerpiece in Ligurian cuisine, should also be of high quality; ask your butcher about organic, ethically raised options.

The following essential ingredients are staples in the Ligurian kitchen and will aid you on your journey into this cuisine:

Anchovies / *Acciughe*:

Although the region by no means lacks access to the sea and therefore an abundance of fresh fish, preserved anchovies have long been a staple of Ligurian cuisine. Before refrigeration, salted, cured anchovies were a favorite because they are long-lasting, flavor-packed, and nutritious. Today you can buy preserved anchovies either packed in salt or oil. The salt-packed variety is superior in flavor but requires rinsing and soaking in cold water for at least fifteen minutes before use. Oil-packed anchovies are essentially the same salt-cured product, but have been pre-rinsed and packed under oil, so they're more convenient to use. For simplicity's sake, I call for oil-packed anchovy fillets in this book, but if you can get your hands on the salt-packed variety and don't mind the extra work involved, I highly recommend them.

Basil / *Basilico*:

Use the freshest, young basil leaves possible, preferably *basilico genovese*. Read more about basil on page 63. Wash and air dry carefully before using; the tender leaves bruise easily. Don't even bother with the dried herb.

Breadcrumbs / *Pan grattato*:

A staple of the inventive, poor cuisines all over Italy (and beyond), breadcrumbs show up frequently in this book's recipes. I recommend making your own from good quality, day-old bread. Simply toast stale bread at 300°F until very dry and blend into a fine powder with a food processor. Freeze until ready to use.

Broth / *Brodo*:

When possible, make your own meat and vegetable broths using kitchen scraps. It is endlessly superior and has a more delicate flavor than the store-bought version. I make a big batch about once a month and freeze it in smaller portions, so I always have some on hand. If you must buy premade broth, opt for a high-quality, low-sodium variety.

Capers / *Capperi*:
Salt-packed capers are more flavorful than the brined ones. Rinse them thoroughly and soak in fresh water for at least fifteen minutes before using.

Chestnut flour / *Farina di castagne*:
Chestnut flour has long been a staple in Liguria, and often substituted wheat flour, which once was a rarer commodity. Now the tables have turned, and chestnut flour is the rarer (and more expensive) of the two. This slightly sweet, earthy flour is versatile and hearty, and stars in both sweet and savory local dishes.

Chickpea flour / *Farina di ceci*:
Also considered as a cheaper and heartier alternative to wheat flour, chickpea flour shows up frequently in Ligurian cuisine, and is the main ingredient of the region's famous street food, *Farinata* (recipe on page 181).

Dried mushrooms / *Funghi secchi*:
Dried mushrooms are one of Ligurian cuisine's secret weapons. They are little umami bombs, often used as a meat-like flavor enhancer for vegetarian dishes. Porcini are undoubtedly the most famous and prized local mushrooms. In the U.S., dried porcini are available in specialty stores and online, but a dried mix of other wild mushrooms make a fine substitute as well. Soak dried mushrooms in warm water for at least twenty minutes before use.

Extra-virgin olive oil / *Olio extravergine d'oliva*:
Seek out Ligurian extra-virgin olive oil from *Taggiasca* olives when possible. If this proves to be difficult or cost-prohibitive, opt for a less expensive but still high-quality and mild-tasting extra-virgin olive oil. Avoid anything in a clear glass bottle because olive oil is sensitive to light and does better when packed in dark bottles or tins. Read more about Ligurian oil on page 154.

Marjoram / *Maggiorana*:

Also known as "*persa*" in local dialect, marjoram is probably the most beloved herb in Liguria, along with basil. Seek it out, and use the fresh herb, not dried, for the recipes in this book.

Oil for frying / *Olio per friggere*:

While Ligurians traditionally fry exclusively with olive oil, most home cooks and restaurants now prefer the more neutral taste (and the friendlier price tag) of vegetable or grapeseed oil.

Olives / *Olive*:

Petit and flavorful Taggiasca are the olives responsible for Liguria's exquisite oil, and they show up in hundreds of local recipes. If you can't get your hands on Taggiasca olives, look for Niçoise, or substitute with Kalamata or your favorite small, flavorful black olive.

Parmigiano-Reggiano cheese / *Parmigiano-Reggiano*:

I urge you to invest in a big chunk of real Parmigiano-Reggiano, preferably aged at least twenty-four months, and grate it yourself as needed. I don't even want to hear about those cheap, convenient, pre-grated, sawdust-like powders. (Cheeses sold as "Parmesan" in the U.S. are not subject to the same kind of regulations that guarantee the quality and origin of Parmigiano-Reggiano.) While freshly grated, real Parmigiano-Reggiano has no equal, an affordable yet acceptable substitute is Grana Padano from Lombardy.

Pasta / *Pasta*:

Buy high-quality, Italian, durum-wheat pasta for the recipes that call for dried pasta in this book. When cooking pasta, make sure to generously salt the water after it comes to a boil; add about two tablespoons salt per gallon of water. Cook pasta until it is just al dente, not mushy. Always set aside a little bit of pasta water before draining; the starchy liquid is your secret weapon for thinning out sauces to the perfect consistency. I usually place a measuring cup in my colander while the pasta is cooking, so I don't forget to take out some water while rushing to drain the pasta.

Rice / *Riso*:
Use short-grain, Italian rice varieties for the risottos in this book, like Arborio or Carnaroli.

Salt / *Sale*:
Use fine-grain sea salt unless otherwise noted. In general, Italians aren't in the habit of using a flaky finishing salt for sprinkling over the final dish, so I haven't called for it in the recipes of this book. However, if you like you may always use your favorite flaky salt to add a crunch and flavor to the finished dish.

Stale bread / *Pane raffermo*:
Being a cuisine based on ingenuity and thrift, a lot Ligurian dishes make use of stale bread. Many of these recipes call for slices of stale white sandwich bread that are soaked in milk or broth before using. If you don't have any stale bread, you may toast a piece of fresh bread in the oven at 300°F until dry.

Stockfish and salt cod / *Stoccafisso e baccalà*:
Preserved cod, whether air-dried as in the case of stockfish, or salt-cured like baccalà, has been popular in Liguria for centuries. They both require long soaking times, but many purveyors now sell them pre-soaked. A well-stocked fishmonger should be able to procure both the dried or pre-soaked fish for you. Read more about stockfish and baccalà, including instructions for soaking them, on page 113.

Antipasti

♦

Appetizers

Compared to other regions of Italy, Liguria does not have an intrinsic tradition of serving appetizers. When I consulted some well-known, older cookbooks from the region, dating back to the 1800s, I noticed they did not dedicate a chapter, not even one recipe, to *antipasti*. Meals began with soup, pasta or rice, and only if you were lucky (i.e., wealthy) was this followed with a second course of fish or meat.

How things have changed. Today, abundance reigns, and appetizers are on the menu of every restaurant in the region. These dishes are often either borrowed from other parts of the country, or were historically considered second courses or side dishes, like *Torta di Riso* (page 167) and *Ripieni di Verdura* (page 145). Ligurians are also expert fryers and will often start a festive meal with a *fritto* or two.

And then, of course, there is *Antipasto Misto*, ubiquitous in family-style trattorias across the countryside. The custom of starting a meal with mixed platters of pickled vegetables, cold cuts, and other crowd-pleasers was imported from neighboring regions but quickly embraced, appropriately adapted to local tastes, and beautifully executed in Liguria as well. (See page 37 for more about *antipasto misto*.)

From the elegant simplicity of marinated anchovies to the hearty comfort of fried dough, after you eat your way through this chapter you will discover how, for a people without a long history of appetizers, Ligurians certainly learned how to do them right.

Salvia Fritta

Fried Sage Leaves

Sage grows bountifully in Liguria but, because of its strong flavor, usually appears in tiny quantities as a flavoring for meats and stews. Here, however, it takes center stage, transformed by the magic of frying into a flavor-packed showstopper. While fried sage leaves aren't unique to this region (you'll find different versions throughout central Italy), it exemplifies the Ligurian penchant for making a meal out of seemingly nothing. In our family, Zia Lidia is the undisputed authority on frying. Her *salvia fritta* is the best I've ever tasted and I shamelessly request it every time I see her. The airy, tempura-like batter is full of secrets, and she has never weighed or measured a single ingredient. So this invaluable recipe has only existed inside her head, until now.

Note: This recipe will make more batter than you need for just the sage leaves, but Zia Lidia insists you don't make a smaller batch because a larger egg-to-flour ratio would make the batter *pesante* (too rich and heavy). However, this is a similar batter to the one used for frying vegetables (page 146), so feel free to slice up an onion or a few zucchini and fry them alongside the sage to use up the extra batter.

♦ Whisk together flour and salt in a wide bowl. Slowly stir in sparkling water, a little at a time, stirring constantly with the whisk; the mixture should have the consistency of thin pancake batter. Whisk vigorously until very smooth; there should be no lumps in sight. Add the egg and stir until well combined. Add the ice cubes and transfer the batter to the refrigerator until ready to fry, up to 2 hours.

Pour about 2 inches of oil into a deep, straight-sided skillet or a wok; heat over high until a drop of batter sizzles and floats to the top when it touches the oil. Working with a few leaves at a time, dip sage in batter, then transfer directly to hot oil. (Important: be VERY CAREFUL not to drop any of the ice cubes into the hot oil; they will explode and send burning oil all over the kitchen and the cook — I speak from experience). Cook until crisp and golden, 2 to 3 minutes. Use a spider or slotted spoon to remove fried leaves from hot oil; transfer to paper towels to drain. Sprinkle with salt and serve hot.

2 cups (9 ounces) all-purpose flour
½ teaspoon salt, plus more to taste
1 ¼ cup sparkling water
1 large egg, lightly beaten
4 ice cubes
Vegetable or grapeseed oil, for frying
35 to 40 fresh sage leaves, washed and patted dry

Serves 4 to 6

Antipasti

Frisceu

Fried Dough

2 cups (9 ounces) all-purpose flour

½ teaspoon active dry yeast

½ teaspoon sugar

⅛ teaspoon salt, plus more for
  serving

1 tablespoon finely diced marjoram or
  sage, or 2 tablespoons finely diced
  spring onion, optional

1 cup plus 1 tablespoon room
  temperature sparkling water
  (you may use tap water in a pinch)

Vegetable or grapeseed oil,
  for frying

Salt to taste

Serves 8 to 10

These puffy, crunchy fried balls of dough are the passion of Ligurian children and adults alike. Paired with a salty anchovy filet or slice of prosciutto they are irresistible in their simplicity. In the local dialect, *frisceu* is a generic term for fritters, both savory and sweet. I love the plain version, but you may add ¼ cup diced spring onion or 2 tablespoons chopped marjoram or sage to the batter, which are popular variations on the classic. I begged our local trattoria, Trattoria Pagliettini, for their secret recipe and they begrudgingly obliged, providing me with the key ingredients and procedure but suspiciously omitting all measurements, claiming they only make it *ad occhio*, or "by eye." The following recipe, the result of painstaking trial and error, will transport you directly into a hilltop trattoria of inland Liguria.

♦   Combine flour, yeast, sugar, and salt in a large bowl; whisk until blended. Add herbs or onion pieces, if using. Slowly pour in the water and stir until smooth. Cover with plastic wrap and set aside to rise until the dough doubles in size, about 1 hour.

Heat 2 inches of oil in a wide, deep straight-sided skillet or wok over medium-high heat until a drop of batter sizzles immediately and floats to the top when it touches the oil. Using two little spoons, drop small (½ teaspoon) balls of dough into the hot oil. Fry, turning occasionally with a spider or slotted spoon, until the balls have puffed and are golden in spots, about 2 to 3 minutes. (*Frisceu* should be crunchy and light beige with golden patches, not dark golden brown.) Transfer the *frisceu* to a paper towel-lined plate, sprinkle with salt to taste, and serve immediately with a glass of crisp vermentino and salty slices of prosciutto or anchovies.

Frisceu di Baccalá

Battered and Fried Salt Cod

2 cups (9 ounces) all-purpose flour

1 teaspoon active dry yeast

1 teaspoon sugar

⅛ teaspoon salt, plus more
for serving

1 ½ cups (12 fluid ounces) room
temperature sparkling water

1 ½ pounds presoaked salt cod,
cut into 1 ½-inch chunks
(see instructions for soaking salt cod
on page 131)

Vegetable or grapeseed oil, for frying

Serves 4 to 6

One of the most popular variations of *frisceu*, these juicy bites of crisp, fried salt cod can be served as a hearty appetizer or as the main dish. If serving as a main, cut the cod into larger (2 ½ inch) chunks.

◆ Combine flour, yeast, sugar, and salt in a large bowl; whisk until blended. Slowly pour in the sparkling water and stir until smooth. Cover with plastic wrap and set aside to rise until the batter almost doubles in size, about 40 to 50 minutes.

Meanwhile, rinse and pat dry the salt cod. Remove the skin and cut the flesh into 1 to 1 ½- inch cubes, removing pin bones as you go.

Heat 3 inches of oil in a wide, deep, straight-sided skillet or wok over medium-high heat until a drop of batter sizzles immediately and floats to the top when it touches the oil. Working in batches, dip the pieces of cod in the batter and transfer to the hot oil. Fry, turning occasionally with a slotted spoon, until the batter has puffed up and is light golden, about 2 to 4 minutes. Transfer to a paper towel-lined plate, taste for salt, and serve immediately.

Cuculli di Ceci

Chickpea Flour Fritters

Chickpea flour is popular in Ligurian cuisine and is the key ingredient in some of my favorite local dishes (see *Panissa* on page 41 and *Farinata* on page 181). Here it is mixed into a batter with yeast and water, and then deep-fried until puffed and golden. These irresistible fried bites are a common way to kick off a meal in the trattorias of Genoa and beyond. They make a great *aperitivo* when served with a glass of sparkling wine.

◆ Combine chickpea flour and yeast in a large bowl, and whisk until blended. Slowly add the water, whisking constantly until smooth. Stir in salt and marjoram. Cover with plastic wrap and set aside to rise until doubled in size, about 1 hour.

Heat 3 inches of oil in a wide, deep, straight-sided skillet or wok over medium-high heat until a drop of batter sizzles immediately and floats to the top when it touches the oil. Using two small spoons, drop small (½ teaspoon) balls of dough into the hot oil. Fry, turning occasionally with a slotted spoon, until the balls are golden, about 3 to 4 minutes. Transfer the *cuculli* to a paper towel-lined plate, sprinkle with salt to taste, and serve immediately.

2 cups (7 oz) chickpea flour

1 ½ teaspoons active dry yeast

1 cup room temperature water

½ teaspoon salt

1 teaspoon finely diced marjoram
   leaves (optional)

Vegetable or grapeseed oil, for frying

Serves 6

Mastering the
Art of Antipasto Misto

In the informal, traditional trattorias that dot the inland hillsides and valleys of Liguria, appetizers are served family-style. "*Antipasto misto*?" the waiter will ask you, and "*Quanti?*" ("How many?"). He doesn't offer any additional information and you don't ask; you simply count how many of your party will be partaking and communicate the number to the server. A short time later, a parade of golden *frisceu*, marinated local mushrooms, multicolored *giardiniera*, thinly sliced prosciutto, and oil-soaked anchovies are arranged in the center of the table, and you fill your plates amidst the loud, chaotic passing of dishes and exuberant pouring of wine. The dishes complement and contrast each other in almost magical harmony: Salty anchovies are mitigated by the pillowy fried dough, while the buttery richness of prosciutto and salami is tempered by the acidity of pickled vegetables.

Make your own antipasto platter. Arrange one or more platters, family style, on the table, including all or some of the following dishes:

♦   Mixed, thinly sliced Italian cold cuts
     (such salami, *prosciutto crudo*, ham, or coppa)
♦   Salt-cured anchovy filets, de-salted and soaked in olive oil
     (see page 21)
♦   *Giardiniera* (page 44)
♦   *Frisceu* (page 33) or *Cuculli di Ceci* (page 35)
♦   *Ripieni di Verdura* (page 145)
♦   *Torte* (pages 157–167)

Condiggiòn

Summer Salad

While this versatile salad can be prepared year round with whatever local produce is in season, it is best enjoyed in the late summer months when garden tomatoes and bell peppers are at their peak. *Condiggiòn* is a close cousin of the French Riviera's Niçoise salad, and also reminiscent of Tuscany's panzanella, thanks to the vinegar-soaked biscuits nestled beneath the vegetables. *Gallette del marinaio* (also known as sea biscuits or hardtack) is the hard, long-lasting bread of Ligurian sailors; make your own with the recipe on page 182, or seek it out in specialty stores. If you can't get your hands on real *gallette del marinaio*, you may substitute with slices of stale or toasted bread. Olive oil-packed tuna, cucumber, boiled potato slices, and other seasonal vegetables are also popular additions to the salad as well.

♦ Bring a medium-sized pot of water to boil over high heat; add a tablespoon of salt. Prepare an ice bath in a large bowl. Cook green beans in boiling water for 5 minutes, or until they are tender but still al dente. Drain green beans and immediately transfer to the ice bath; let cool for 5 minutes. Drain beans again and set them aside to dry.

Prepare a wide, shallow salad bowl. Cut the garlic in half lengthwise and vigorously rub the inside of the bowl with the cut side of the garlic.

If using *gallette del marinaio:* Rub the *gallette* with the cut side of the garlic clove; set aside garlic for another use. Stir together 1 cup water, ½ teaspoon salt, and 2 tablespoons of vinegar in a wide bowl, and add *gallette*. Set aside for 2 to 3 minutes until the *gallette* are softened. Drain and squeeze them gently with your hands to remove excess liquid. Tear into bite-sized chunks and add to the salad bowl.

If using stale or toasted bread: Rub the bread with the cut side of the garlic clove; set aside garlic for another use. Tear or cut bread into bite-sized chunks and add to the salad bowl. Sprinkle with 1 tablespoon vinegar, 1 tablespoon olive oil, and a pinch of salt.

Add green beans, tomatoes, red onion, bell pepper, olives, and anchovies to the salad bowl. Tear 8 of the basil leaves in half with your hands and add to the salad. Drizzle salad with about 3 tablespoons of olive oil and 1 to 2 tablespoons of vinegar (adjusted according to taste). Sprinkle with a generous pinch of salt and toss gently. Cover the salad and set aside at room temperature for at least 15 minutes or up to an hour. Taste and adjust seasonings before serving.

Divide salad between 4 plates, top with hard-boiled egg pieces, garnish with remaining basil leaves, and serve immediately.

2 cups green beans, trimmed and
   halved crosswise

Salt to taste

1 clove garlic

4 *gallette del marinaio* (sea biscuits),
   or 4 slices of stale or toasted bread

Extra-virgin olive oil to taste

Red wine vinegar to taste

2 ½ cups coarsely chopped fresh
   tomatoes (beefsteak, heirloom,
   or cherry tomatoes are all
   nice options)

1 small red onion, thinly sliced

1 yellow or orange bell pepper,
   thinly sliced

¼ cup Taggiasche or Niçoise olives

4 to 6 oil-packed anchovy fillets,
   cut in half crosswise

16 fresh basil leaves

3 hard-boiled eggs, peeled and
   quartered

Serves 4

Panissa

Chickpea Batter

Not to be confused with the Piemontese rice dish of the same name, Ligurian *panissa* is best described as stiff polenta made out of chickpea flour. After about 25 minutes of slow-cooking and constant stirring (arm yourself with patience and a kitchen stool for this one), the thick mixture is poured into a shallow bowl, chilled, then cut into slices, sticks, or cubes. At this point, it can be dressed with olive oil and vinegar and served in a salad, sautéed with onions and served warm, or (my favorite) fried until crisp and served piping hot with lots of salt (recipes on page 42).

◆　Pour the chickpea flour and salt into a large, heavy-bottomed saucepan or nonstick pot. Stir with a whisk to break up any lumps. Slowly pour in about 1 cup of the water and whisk until smooth. Continue adding the rest of the water, a little at a time, stirring constantly with the whisk to avoid forming lumps. Set aside to rest for 30 minutes.

Prepare a few shallow bowls into which you will pour the *panissa* by brushing the insides with a light veil of olive oil, and set aside.

Place the pot containing the chickpea mixture over medium heat and cook, stirring constantly. As soon as the mixture begins to thicken (after about 10 minutes), reduce the heat to low. When the mixture becomes too dense to stir with the whisk, switch to a wooden spoon. Continue to cook, stirring constantly, until mixture is very thick and the spoon leaves a trail, about 25 to 30 minutes. Remove from heat and immediately pour the mixture into prepared bowls, about 1 inch deep. Let cool at room temperature for 30 minutes, then cover with plastic wrap, pressing it directly onto the surface of the *panissa*. Refrigerate for at least 2 hours, or preferably about 8 hours.

Remove the *panissa* from the refrigerator and discard plastic wrap. Invert bowls onto a cutting board and slice the *panissa* into desired shapes.

3 cups (about 10 ½ ounces)
　chickpea flour
1 ½ teaspoons salt
4 ¼ cups water
Extra-virgin olive oil for greasing bowls

Serves 4 to 6

Panissa Fritta

Fried Panissa

The best fried *panissa* I've ever tasted came out of a cozy, one-room *gastronomia* (deli) in the tiny beach town of Cavi Borgo. Alberto and Caterina turn out handmade ravioli, *Pansoti* (see page 81), pasta sauces, savory pies, and other delicacies for the tourists in the summer and the (very few) locals left behind in the winter. Caterina taught me to cut the *panissa* into the shape of French fries for optimum frying and presentation: The form and color are familiar, yet the taste and texture delightfully new. Alternatively, *panissa fritta* is often thinly sliced, resulting in an extra crispy, almost chip-like final product, though slices are a little harder to handle than matchsticks, and sometimes break apart while frying.

1 recipe *Panissa* (see page 41), chilled and cut into desired shapes
Vegetable or grapeseed oil, for frying

Serves 4 to 6

♦ Cut the *panissa* into French-fry shaped sticks or thin slices, as desired. Keep the cut *panissa* in the refrigerator until ready to fry. Heat about 2 inches of oil in a wide, deep, straight-sided skillet or wok over medium-high heat. To test if the oil is ready, toss a crumb of bread into the oil; if it sizzles and floats to the top immediately, it's time to fry. Fry *panissa* in small batches, turning occasionally, until golden and crisp, 2 to 4 minutes. Remove from oil with a spider or slotted spoon and transfer to a paper towel-lined tray. Sprinkle with salt to taste and serve hot.

Insalata di Panissa

Panissa Salad

1 recipe *Panissa* (see page 41), chilled and cut into cubes
⅓ cup Taggiasche or Niçoise olives, pitted
2 celery stalks, thinly sliced crosswise
1 small red onion, thinly sliced
Juice from 1 lemon
2 tablespoons diced flat-leaf parsley
2 tablespoons extra-virgin olive oil, or more to taste
Salt and pepper, to taste

Serves 4

While *panissa*'s most common street food iteration is fried (see above), I love it in this fresh salad form as well. Serve small salads as an appetizer, or bigger portions as a protein-packed vegetarian main.

♦ Place the panissa, olives, celery, and onion in a large bowl. Add lemon juice, parsley, olive oil, salt, and pepper to taste. Serve cold or at room temperature.

Giardiniera

Mixed Pickled Vegetables

This simple mix of pickled garden vegetables is popular all over Italy, and Liguria is no exception. It's a key player in the *Antipasto Misto* (see page 37), along with prosciutto crudo and anchovies, that you'll find in most inland trattorias. *Giardiniera* was designed to preserve abundant summer produce at its peak, so choose a colorful array of vegetables that are fresh, ripe, and in season. The best way to ensure each vegetable is perfectly cooked is to boil them separately in the vinegar solution, transfer them to an ice bath with a slotted spoon when they're perfectly al dente, then start over with the next vegetable. Admittedly, I never do it that way because it takes forever, so I've included the timing for cooking mixed vegetables all together here.

♦   First, prepare your vegetables and keep them separate: cut carrots, zucchini, and cucumber into ¼-inch-thick rounds; break cauliflower into small, bite-sized florets; slice bell peppers into thin strips; peel garlic cloves and keep them whole; trim green beans and cut them in half crosswise; cut celery into bite-sized chunks; cut radishes into 4 spears. Pearl onions should be peeled and (depending on their size) used whole, halved, or quartered.

Combine vinegar, white wine, water, sugar, salt, bay leaves, and peppercorns in a large pot and bring to a boil over high heat. Add the hardest vegetables first: carrots, cauliflower, and celery. When the solution comes back to a boil, set timer for 2 minutes, then add bell peppers, green beans, and zucchini. Cook for another 2 minutes after the water comes back to a simmer, then add cucumbers, pearl onions, and radishes. Boil for a final 3 minutes.

Fill a large bowl with ice water. Using a spider or slotted spoon, transfer the cooked vegetables to an ice bath. Let cool for 5 minutes, then drain the vegetables. Set aside vinegar solution to cool.

If you will be canning your *giardiniera* for longer shelf life, sterilize your jars now.

Fill jars evenly with the cooked vegetables, leaving about ½-inch headspace. Pour cooled vinegar solution over the vegetables, covering them completely but leaving at least ¼ inch headspace. Close jars tightly with lids.

If you are canning the *giardiniera*, process your jars in a boiling water bath now, let cook for 20 minutes, and then store at room temperature. Otherwise, transfer your jars to the refrigerator.

You can eat the *giardiniera* right away, but it gets better with time, so I recommend waiting 5 to 7 days before serving.

If canned in sterilized jars, the *giardiniera* can be stored at room temperature in a dry, dark place for up to a year. Otherwise it will keep in the refrigerator for up to 3 weeks.

3 pounds mixed fresh vegetables (such as carrots, zucchini, cucumbers, cauliflower florets, bell peppers, green beans, garlic cloves, celery, radishes, and pearl or baby onions)

3 cups white wine vinegar

1 ½ cups dry white wine

3 cups water

⅓ cup sugar

2 tablespoons salt

3 bay leaves

1 tablespoon whole black peppercorns

6 wide mouth, 1-pint jars with lids

Makes six 1-pint jars

Brandacujùn

"Shaken" Stockfish and Potato Spread

Popular in Ponente, *Brandacujùn* is a traditional sailor's dish, born on long voyages when potatoes, stockfish, and naughty language were the only things in abundant supply. A composite of the verb *brandare*, which means "to shake," and *cujun*, a vulgar term for testicle, the name of this dish keeps scholars guessing and children giggling to this day. One popular explanation for the colorful moniker is that the ship's cook would sit down to shake the pot vigorously on his lap as the last step of the recipe requires, giving his family jewels quite a jiggle in the process.

4 medium, floury potatoes

Salt

1 ½ pounds pre-soaked stockfish or salt cod (see instructions for soaking on page 113)

1 tablespoon white-wine vinegar

½ cup plus 1 tablespoon extra-virgin olive oil, divided

1 clove of garlic, finely grated or minced

1 tablespoon finely chopped flat-leaf parsley

¼ teaspoon freshly ground white pepper

1 tablespoon freshly squeezed lemon juice

2 tablespoons pine nuts, roughly chopped

Crostini or toasted slices of baguette, for serving

Serves 4

♦ Scrub the potatoes and place them in a large pot. Cover with 1 inch of cold water, add 2 tablespoons salt, and bring to a boil over high heat. Lower heat to maintain a simmer until a fork meets no resistance when poked into the potatoes, but before they are so soft they begin to break apart easily. Drain potatoes and set aside until cool enough to handle, then peel and chop them into bite-sized pieces.

Meanwhile, cut the fish into 2-inch strips and place in a large saucepan full of cold water. Add 1 tablespoon of salt (if using salt cod omit the salt) and 1 tablespoon of vinegar; bring to a boil over medium-high heat. Boil for 15 minutes; drain and set aside until cool enough to handle. Remove skin and pin bones; dice the flesh into tiny pieces.

Combine ½ cup olive oil, garlic, parsley, white pepper, and lemon juice in a small bowl, stir vigorously to combine. Heat the remaining 1 tablespoon of olive oil in a large saucepan with a tightly fitting lid. When the oil is shimmering, add the chopped fish and stir to coat. Add the potatoes and pine nuts, stir until warmed through, then turn off the heat. Taste for salt and add more if necessary. Pour in parsley mixture and cover the saucepan tightly with lid. Cover the lid and sides of the pot with a dishcloth and, holding the lid firmly closed with your hands, swirl quickly in a circular motion, stopping after each couple of turns to shake the contents back and forth a few times. Check the mixture frequently; the potatoes should be creamy and well combined with the fish, but not quite the consistency of mashed potatoes; there should still be chunks of potato and fish visible. (Alternatively, you may stir the mixture vigorously with a wooden spoon until you reach the desired consistency.) Taste, then adjust salt and other seasonings to taste.

Serve at room temperature with crostini or toasted slices of baguette.

Acciughe Marinate

Marinated Fresh Anchovies

A staple in Liguria, anchovies usually make an appearance at least once in the course of a typical meal, whether fresh, cured, fried, baked, stewed, or pickled. If you're put off by the salty brown fillets common in the U.S., this elegant preparation of these tiny silver fish may well change your mind. In this charming appetizer, surprising in its simplicity, the fresh fish is cured in a vinegar and lemon solution, and the delicate result is a far cry from what you find in a tin. Note: The fish in this recipe is marinated, but raw, so buying freshly-frozen anchovies, or deep-freezing the fillets for at least 96 hours after cleaning, is highly recommended for food safety.

♦ Clean and fillet anchovies following the instructions on page 104. Rinse well and arrange in a single layer in a deep, wide dish. Stir together lemon juice, vinegar, and salt; pour mixture over fish. Cover with plastic wrap and refrigerate at least 4 hours, or up to 48 hours. Before serving, drain fish and discard marinade. Arrange on a serving dish and drizzle with 1 or 2 tablespoons olive oil. Sprinkle with parsley and red pepper flakes if using. Serve lightly chilled.

1 pound whole, fresh anchovies
   (about 25)
½ cup fresh lemon juice
½ cup white wine vinegar
1 teaspoon salt
1 to 2 tablespoons extra-virgin olive oil
1 tablespoon very finely chopped flat
   leaf parsley
Red pepper flakes (optional)

Serves 4

Barbagiuai

Uncle Giovanni's Fried Pumpkin Ravioli

For the pasta:

2 cups (9 ounces) bread flour

¼ cup room temperature water

¼ cup dry white wine

2 tablespoons extra-virgin olive oil,
  plus more for brushing

½ teaspoon salt

For the filling:

1 tablespoon extra-virgin olive oil

1 leek, white and light green part only,
  finely diced

1 cup (9 ounces) pumpkin purée,
  canned or homemade

¼ cup cooked white rice

1 ½ ounces finely grated Parmigiano-
  Reggiano (about ½ cup, packed)

⅓ cup whole milk ricotta

1 large egg, lightly beaten

1 teaspoon finely chopped marjoram

¼ teaspoon salt

To finish:

Vegetable or grapeseed oil, for frying

Serves 4 to 6

Somewhere near Camporosso, in the farthest western reaches of Liguria, somebody's uncle at some point made these fried delights famous. *Barbagiuai* literally means "Uncle Giovanni," though it's unclear who he was, besides a genius in the kitchen. A slightly sweet pumpkin and cheese filling is encased in a wine-spiked dough and fried until crisp, golden, and irresistible. Remember to get a head start on this recipe; the shaped ravioli need to dry out at room temperature for a couple of hours before frying. This filling is also delicious inside traditional, unfried ravioli. Try substituting it for the vegetable filling in the *Ravioli di Magro* recipe (page 73).

◆   For the pasta: Combine flour, water, and wine in the bowl of a stand mixer fitted with a dough hook. Knead on medium-low speed until a shaggy dough forms, about 5 minutes. Add olive oil and salt and continue kneading until dough is soft, smooth, and elastic, another 5 to 7 minutes. Remove from mixer, form into a ball, and wrap tightly in plastic wrap. Let rest at room temperature for 30 minutes. Remove plastic wrap (do not discard) and cut the dough equally into 6 pieces. Cover the pieces with the plastic wrap to keep them from drying out, and let rest for another 10 minutes.

Meanwhile, make the filling: Heat the olive oil in a large skillet over medium-high heat. Add the leek and sauté until soft, about 5 minutes. Add the pumpkin purée and cook, stirring until all liquid has evaporated and mixture is fragrant, 2 to 3 minutes. Transfer mixture to a medium-sized bowl and let cool slightly. When the mixture has cooled, add cooked rice, Parmigiano-Reggiano, ricotta, egg, marjoram, and salt. Mix well.

◆   To fill the pasta: If desired, transfer the mixture to a pastry bag with a wide, round tip.

Continued...

Roll out 1 rectangular sheet of pasta as thinly as possible following the instructions on page 60. Lay pasta sheet on a floured surface and distribute small mounds of filling at regular intervals along one lengthwise half of the sheet; use about 1 teaspoon of filling for each mound. The mounds should be 2 inches apart from each other in a straight line, at least ¾ of an inch from the edge of the pasta sheet. Moisten the other half of the dough with a pastry brush dipped in water. Carefully lift the moistened dough and fold it over the other half of the dough, covering the mounds of filling. Press around the filling with your fingertips to seal the pasta and remove any air pockets. Cut in a straight line between each mound of filling with a knife or ravioli cutter. The finished ravioli should be about 2 ½ by 3 inches. As a precaution, press again around the edges of the individual ravioli with your fingertips to be sure they're completely sealed. Transfer ravioli to a tray lined with a clean, flour-dusted kitchen towel; be careful not to let them overlap, or they will stick together. Repeat with remaining pasta and filling. Let ravioli rest, uncovered, at room temperature at least 2 hours, and up to 4 hours.

Heat oil in a wide, deep, straight-sided skillet or a wok, until a pinch of breadcrumbs or flour tossed into the hot oil sizzles upon contact. Fry the ravioli in batches, without crowding the pan, until golden, puffed, and crunchy. Transfer to a paper towel-lined plate with a spider or slotted spoon and repeat with remaining ravioli. Sprinkle with salt to taste and serve immediately.

Primi

◆

Pasta, Risotto & Soups

Pastas, soups, risottos, ravioli, gnocchi ... in general, Italians excel when it comes to *primi piatti*, and Liguria is no different. Since the late 1700s, first courses, comprised of endless variations of soups, rice, and pasta dishes, have played a central role on the Ligurian table, regardless of wealth and class.

My husband's aunt, Zia Marghe, loaned me a leather-bound, original edition of the 1865 cookbook *La Vera Cucina Genovese* (*Real Genovese Cuisine*) when I began research for this book. As I studied the yellowing, crumbling pages, I was struck, not only by the antiquated Italian but also by the unusual recipe organization. The first course, too massive to group into one chapter, was split into four: *minestre e zuppe di grasso* (meat soups), *minestre e zuppe di magro* (non-meat soups), *minestre asciutte condite di grasso* ("dry soups," which included rice, pasta dishes, and gnocchi) with meat, and *minestre asciutte condite di magro* (dry soups without meat).

One reason for their popularity here is that *primi*, especially pasta and rice, serve as a hearty blank canvas that takes full advantage of Liguria's best ingredients: vegetables, herbs, and extra-virgin olive oil. The now world-famous pesto, invented in Liguria, is a perfect example. Basil, pine nuts, cheese, and olive oil by themselves would make for a meager meal, but when smashed together and tossed with pasta, a beautiful, flavorful, and substantial dish is born.

From homemade pasta with that world-famous basil sauce, to the lesser known stuffed lettuce soup, and ubiquitous ravioli, these resourceful recipes are the perfect way to showcase the raw ingredients that thrive in the region.

Corzetti

Ligurian Stamped Pasta

A Ligurian tradition dating back to the Middle Ages, it is said that this disk-shaped pasta was originally embossed using a medieval coin called a *corzetto*, which was later replaced by special, hand-carved wooden stamps. During the Renaissance, noble families would have their coat of arms stamped into pasta for special occasions. The two-part tool is a work of art itself, comprised of a concave cutter and an elaborately engraved stamp. A visit to the workshop of one of the few local *intagliatori* (woodcarvers) that still engrave custom *corzetti* stamps is an inspiring experience. In the U.S., seek out *corzetti* stamps online, in specialty kitchen stores like Williams Sonoma, or order them directly from a family of Tuscan woodcarvers (*romagnolipastatools. com*). Dress the cooked *corzetti* with extra virgin olive oil, toasted pine nuts, freshly grated Parmigiano-Reggiano, and fresh marjoram. Alternatively, you can serve with sauce of choice like pesto (page 66 or 67), *Tócco* (page 126), or *Salsa di Noci* (page 83).

♦ Sift together the flours. Combine flours, eggs, and ¼ cup wine in a food processor fitted with a metal blade. Process for 30 to 60 seconds. If the dough doesn't come together, add another teaspoon of wine and process again. Repeat as necessary until dough comes together in a rough, shaggy ball. (Alternatively, you may mix the dough by hand, following the instructions on page 60.) Remove the dough from the food processor and transfer to a clean work surface. Knead by hand for a few minutes until it comes together into a smooth ball (only flour the work surface if the dough is sticking). Form a ball, wrap tightly with plastic wrap, and let rest at room temperature for 30 minutes to 2 hours.

Roll out the dough according to the instructions on page 60. The pasta should be thin, but thick enough to hold up to the embossing, about 2 mm (¹⁄₁₆-inch). Cut out as many rounds as possible using the concave, cutter part of the *corzetti* stamp. To emboss: Place one round of pasta dough on the embosser part of the stamp, pressing to adhere. Place the handle of the stamp over the pasta round and press firmly. Transfer stamped *corzetti* to a semolina-dusted kitchen towel. Do not overlap or they might stick together. Repeat with remaining rounds. You may cook *corzetti* immediately or leave it out to dry for a few hours before cooking.

Cook *corzetti* in a large pot of generously salted water until al dente, 5 to 7 minutes, depending on the thickness of the pasta. Drain (remember to reserve some cooking water to thin out your sauce, if needed) and dress *corzetti* with desired sauce. Serve immediately.

1 ¼ cups (7 oz) semolina flour,
  plus more for dusting
1 ½ cups (6.75 oz) all-purpose flour,
  plus more for dusting
3 large eggs
¼ cup dry white wine, or as needed
Salt
Sauce of choice, for serving

Special equipment:
Corzetti stamp (see note, above)

Serves 4 to 6

Picagge Verdi

Green "Ribbons"

In the Genovese dialect, *picagge* means "cotton ribbons," in reference to this handmade pasta's wide, flat format. Similar to tagliatelle, the dough is rolled out by hand or with a pasta maker and then cut into broad strips up to two-inches wide. In this popular variation, the noodles are tinted green by borage leaves blended into the dough. Borage, also known as starflower, is a wild herb native to the Mediterranean. It has a fresh, cucumber-like taste and surfaces frequently in Ligurian cuisine. If you can't get your hands on fresh borage, feel free to substitute with a mix of greens. Serve with *Tócco* sauce (page 126), tomato sauce, or simply extra-virgin olive oil and freshly grated Parmigiano-Reggiano.

♦ Bring a large pot of water to boil, then add 2 tablespoons salt. Prepare an ice water bath. Trim borage leaves. Cook the leaves in the boiling water until softened, about 3 minutes. Drain and transfer immediately to ice water. Let cool for a few minutes, then drain, and wring out excess moisture. Finely chop the borage with a knife or in a food processor.

Pour the flour into a mound in the center of a large work surface. Make a well in the center and crack the eggs into it. Stir eggs with a fork, without touching the flour, until yolks are combined with whites. Stir in the borage and begin incorporating bits of the flour from the walls of the well with your fingertips. Continue to work in more flour until it is all combined and a shaggy, sticky mass has formed. At this point the dough won't look very promising, but don't get discouraged! Begin kneading and folding with your hands until the dough becomes satiny and elastic, about 10 minutes. If the dough is still sticky after 10 minutes, sprinkle with a bit more flour and continue kneading until smooth. Alternatively, you may knead in a stand mixer with the dough hook for about 5 minutes. Form into a ball, wrap tightly with plastic wrap, and rest at room temperature for 30 minutes or up to 2 hours. (At this point, you may refrigerate the dough for up to 24 hours; bring to room temperature before rolling.)

Cut a fist-sized portion of dough and roll it into a thin sheet (the second-to-thinnest setting on a pasta machine) following the instructions on page 60, taking care to cover the remaining dough with plastic wrap so it doesn't dry out in the meantime. Cut into 1-inch ribbons and set them aside on a clean, flour-dusted kitchen towel; do not overlap the noodles. Repeat with remaining dough.

Cook pasta in boiling, generously salted water until al dente, 4 to 6 minutes. Drain, reserving about a cup of the cooking water, and serve with desired sauce (thinning it first with reserved cooking water as needed), or simply toss with extra-virgin olive oil and freshly grated Parmigiano-Reggiano.

Salt

4 ½ cups (10 ½ ounces) loosely packed borage leaves (you may substitute with *Preboggión* —
see page 78 — or a mix of chopped beet tops and Swiss chard)

3 cups (13 ½ ounces) all-purpose flour

3 large eggs

4 to 6 servings

Pasta Fresca Ligure

Ligurian Fresh Pasta Sheets

In a land defined by frugality, eggs were a luxury not to be squandered. So, it's no surprise that the traditional Ligurian recipes contain few, if any, eggs, as compared to the richer, nearly orange-colored, pastas of Emilia-Romagna. As an American, I tend to assume that more is better, and originally thought that the low egg-to-flour ratio was a historic error that needed to be fixed. Over time (and many plates of pasta) I discovered that this paler Ligurian pasta has a more delicate taste that really lets the sauce or the filling take center stage. After mixing many batches by hand, I have also discovered that a food processor is my favorite tool for making the dough. It comes together in just a few minutes and the results are soft and subtle, though I'm not sure *nonna* would approve of the shortcut.

◆ Food processor: Combine flour, eggs, and ½ cup water in a food processor fitted with a metal blade. Process for 30 to 60 seconds. If the dough doesn't come together, add another teaspoon of water and process again. Repeat until dough comes together in a rough, shaggy ball. Transfer to a clean work surface. Knead by hand for a minute or two until it comes together into a smooth ball. If the dough is too sticky, sprinkle with a bit more flour and continue kneading until smooth. (The dough might feel a little tight, but it will become more elastic as it rests.)

◆ Hand mixing: Pour the flour in a mound in the center of a large work surface. Make a well in the center and crack the eggs into it. Add 6 tablespoons water to eggs and stir with a fork, without incorporating the flour, until frothy. Begin incorporating bits of flour from the walls of the well with your fingertips and add 2 more tablespoons of water. Continue to work in more flour until it is all combined and a shaggy, sticky mass has formed. Add more water, 1 teaspoon at a time, if dough isn't coming together. Begin kneading and folding with your hands until the dough becomes satiny and elastic, about 10 minutes. If the dough is still sticky, sprinkle with a bit more flour and continue kneading until smooth. (The dough might feel a little tight, but it will become more elastic as it rests.)

◆ To finish: Form a ball, wrap tightly with plastic wrap and let rest at room temperature for 30 minutes to 1 hour. (At this point, you may refrigerate the dough for up to 24 hours; bring to room temperature before rolling.) Roll out.

Roll out the dough with a pasta maker, or with a rolling pin on a flour-dusted surface. Working in batches, cut fist-sized portions of dough and roll as thinly

4 cups (18 ounces) flour
  (preferably 00)
2 large eggs
½ cup room temperature water,
  or more as necessary

Serves 4 to 6
  (makes about 1 ½ pounds pasta)

as possible; cover the remaining dough with plastic wrap so it doesn't dry out in the meantime. If you're using a pasta maker, roll the dough through the largest setting, fold it into thirds and repeat the process 2 times. Now you may begin rolling the dough thinner; turn the dial to the next narrowest setting and feed the sheet through the rollers. Dust pasta and rollers with flour as necessary to keep it from sticking. Keep reducing the settings until the dough is rolled to desired thickness.

Mandìlli de Sæa

Silk Handkerchiefs

Making *Mandìlli de Sæa* (in dialect "silk handkerchiefs") at home is rare nowadays, since it requires patience and skill to roll the pasta sheet into a translucent veil without tearing it. These impossibly thin, silky pasta squares are often served at Christmas dinner or other special occasions. My mother-in-law buys them at her favorite deli in the *carruggi* (alleyways) of Genoa on Christmas Eve, and they are always part of the evening's menu, served with freshly made pesto. Pay close attention to the cooking instructions here: You'll need to boil only a few "handkerchiefs" at a time and pull them out of the water with a slotted spoon to avoid them sticking and tearing during the cooking and draining process.

♦ Cut a fist-sized portion of dough and roll as thinly as possible. If you are using a pasta maker, roll to the narrowest setting and feed the sheet through it twice, then roll by hand a few times to make it even thinner. Ideally, the sheet will be translucent, and you should be able to see your hand through the pasta. Cut the sheet into 5-inch squares and set them aside on a clean, flour-dusted kitchen towel, being careful not to overlap or they will stick together. Repeat with remaining dough.

Bring a wide pot of water to boil, salt generously, and add 1 tablespoon of olive oil. Scoop pesto into a small bowl; set aside. Prepare individual plates for each person. Cook only 3 to 4 pasta squares at a time in boiling water, until tender but still al dente, about 1 minute. Stir a tablespoon or two of cooking water into the pesto in order to thin out the sauce slightly. Using a spider or slotted spoon, transfer the cooked pasta to a serving plate. Stack the sheets on top of each other, dolloping a teaspoon of pesto between each sheet. Repeat with remaining pasta and pesto, distributing evenly between plates. Top with a final spoonful of pesto. Serve immediately with freshly grated Parmigiano-Reggiano.

1 recipe *Pasta Fresca Ligure*
  (see page 60)
1 tablespoon extra-virgin olive oil
1 cup homemade pesto
  (either *Pesto Tradizionale* on page 66
  or *Pesto nel Mixer* on page 67)
Finely grated Parmigiano-Reggiano, for
  serving

Serves 4 to 6

Basilico Genovese

Genovese Basil

To say that Ligurians are particular about their basil is an understatement. The scrutiny the poor plant endures here borders on mania, especially where pesto is concerned. Over the years, I've often observed our *nonne* in the kitchen, sniffing a sprig of the bright green herb purchased at the market. Nine out of ten times, they wrinkle their noses and declare, disapprovingly, *"Sa di menta"*—it smells like mint. This is the ultimate insult for basil; it means the plant is too mature, that the tender leaves have lost the delicate, sweet flavor of their youth and assumed the more pungent, mint-like flavor of older plants.

The local, round-leafed variety, *basilico genovese*, is renowned for its sweet, mild flavor and is protected under strict DOP regulations. To understand more about this prized plant, I visited Paolo Calcagno's commercial basil farm: an ambitious, nearly vertical, hillside operation west of Genoa. His numerous greenhouses, carpeted with electric green seedlings, overlook the sea, as do all the greenhouses in the area. The microclimate of these hills combined with the sun and the salty sea air provide the optimum growing conditions for the herb.

Paolo showed me how they grow and collect basil according to the DOP guidelines. The tiny plants are harvested when they are only about a month old, six inches tall, and have only sprouted four to six leaves. Pickers lounge on wooden planks suspended inches above the tender leaves, and carefully pluck the plants out of the soil from their stems, one at a time, roots and all. The plants are then gathered into bouquets, the roots bound and wrapped in bright pink paper. "Hot pink is our color," he grinned as he passed me a perfumed bouquet of freshly picked plants, "it looks so pretty with the bright green leaves."

I stuck my nose into the bouquet and was intoxicated by the perfect scent. *This* is what basil is supposed to smell like: floral with a hint of pepper and a sweet, clove-like aroma ... and not a hint of mint.

You don't have to travel to Italy to try *basilico genovese*, however: seeds are available in the States, and it is easy to grow. Plants will grow in pots inside all year-round if you keep them in a sunny spot. Just remember to harvest the leaves when they are still small and tender, or a *nonna* somewhere will wrinkle her nose in disapproval.

Pesto Tradizionale

Traditional Pesto

3 cups (2 ½ ounces) tightly packed,
   fresh, small basil leaves,
   stems removed

1 large or 2 small cloves of garlic, halved
   and inner green germ removed

¼ cup (1.2 ounces) pine nuts

¼ teaspoon coarse sea salt

1 cup, packed (3 ½ ounces) finely
   grated Parmigiano-Reggiano

⅓ cup, packed (1 ounce) finely grated
   pecorino, preferably Fiore Sardo

½ cup extra-virgin olive oil, plus more as
   needed

Special equipment:
Mortar and pestle

Makes about 1 ⅓ cup, enough for
   8 servings

The first time I tasted *real* pesto in Liguria, made in a mortar and pestle, I couldn't believe my palate. It was beyond delicious, a completely different experience from the packaged, or even made-in-a-food-processor versions I tasted in the past.

Undoubtedly the most iconic dish of Liguria, pesto has made quite the journey since its humble beginnings. It is now wildly popular, in some form or another, the world over. However, I have to agree with the locals: It's nearly impossible to eat a decent pesto outside the region, much less outside of the country. Even within Liguria, no two pestos are alike. The recipe varies from valleys to hilltops, from mother to child, from brother to sister. In Moneglia, my mother-in-law and her two sisters, who grew up in the same house and learned to cook from the same women, make three completely different pestos: one is creamier, one is heavier on the basil, one is chunkier. Whose is the correct one is a fiercely contested matter.

What all Ligurians do agree upon is that you should ideally prepare pesto in a mortar and pestle and seek out the absolute best ingredients: the sweetest, Italian pine nuts, the youngest, most tender basil leaves grown in and around Pra, outside Genoa, Ligurian extra-virgin olive oil from prized Taggiasche olives, Parmigiano-Reggiano aged over 24 months, and a perfect pecorino Fiore Sardo (a slightly smoky, raw sheep's milk cheese from Sardinia). While Ligurians are ferocious about fine quality of ingredients, they are also a thrifty folk, so while frowned upon, walnuts are a permitted substitution for pine nuts by the official local guidelines.

Arm yourself with patience and strong biceps for this recipe; the result is well worth the effort.

♦ Gently wash the basil in a tub of cold water, being careful not to bruise or smash it. Drain carefully and transfer to a clean kitchen towel to air dry or use a salad spinner. Using a mortar and pestle, grind garlic into a paste. Add pine nuts and continue to crush and mix with the pestle until finely ground. Add about half of the basil leaves and the salt. Grind (don't pound) the mixture against the interior walls of the mortar in a circular motion into a smooth paste. The basil leaves should be finely shredded, not smashed or bruised. Add the other half of the basil leaves and continue grinding into a thick, dark green paste. Stir in both cheeses, then slowly drizzle in the olive oil, stirring constantly with the pestle until you obtain a bright green, creamy sauce. Add more oil, if desired, for a smoother consistency.

Serve over pasta of your choice (see page 60 or 61 for recipes), being sure to thin the sauce first with a bit of the pasta cooking water. Alternatively, scoop pesto into a container and cover with a layer of olive oil to prevent oxidation. Cover and refrigerate for up to 2 days or freeze for up to 3 months.

Pesto nel Mixer

Pesto in a Food Processor

All of Liguria agrees: Pesto prepared in a food processor is an undeniably inferior product, but everyone does it. My friend Enrica Monzani, who was once a finalist at the World Pesto Championship, let me in on some of her secrets. The main problem with blenders and food processors is that the metal blades tend to overheat the tender basil leaves and cause oxidation, altering the final product's flavor and color. To avoid this, chill the bowl and blades of a food processor in the freezer for 15 minutes, and refrigerate the olive oil for at least 30 minutes before preparing the pesto. Enrica prefers to use an immersion blender with a carafe, which works beautifully even with small portions of pesto. Big food processors do better with big batches, so consider doubling or tripling the recipe if that is your only option, and freezing the extra pesto for future use.

3 cups (2 ½ ounces) tightly packed, fresh, small basil leaves, stems removed

½ cup extra-virgin olive oil, plus more as needed

1 large or 2 small cloves of garlic, halved and inner green germ removed

¼ cup (1.2 ounces) pine nuts

¼ teaspoon salt

1 cup, packed (3 ½ ounces) finely grated Parmigiano-Reggiano

⅓ cup, packed (1 ounce) finely grated pecorino, preferably Fiore Sardo

Makes about 1 ⅓ cup

♦ Gently wash the basil in a tub of cold water, being careful not to bruise or smash it. Drain carefully and transfer to a clean kitchen towel to air dry or use a salad spinner. Chill the bowl and blades of a food processor in the freezer for 15 minutes and refrigerate the olive oil for at least 30 minutes before preparing the pesto. Combine garlic, pine nuts, salt, and 2 tablespoons of olive oil in the bowl of a food processor and blend until finely minced. Add basil and 2 more tablespoons of olive oil and pulse until basil is finely chopped. Add grated cheeses, 2 more tablespoons of olive oil, and pulse until mixture is well combined and begins to look creamy; transfer to a bowl. Drizzle in the remaining oil, stirring constantly with a wooden spoon, until creamy and well combined. Add more oil as needed to reach desired consistency and adjust salt to taste.

Serve over pasta of your choice (see page 60 or 61 for recipes), being sure to thin the sauce first with a bit of the pasta cooking water. Alternatively, scoop pesto into a container and cover with a layer of olive oil to prevent oxidation. Cover and refrigerate for up to 2 days or freeze for up to 3 months.

Trenette al Pesto con fagiolini e Patate

Trenette with Pesto, Green Beans, and Potatoes

Local *nonne* will toss the potatoes, green beans, and pasta for this recipe in the boiling water in sequence; they know by experience when to add in each one. Seeing as pasta cooking times vary greatly, I tend to cook the vegetables and pasta separately; it takes a little bit longer but ensures optimum consistency of each one. Try substituting zucchini matchsticks for the green beans for another popular variation.

Salt

9 ounces (about 2 cups) green beans, trimmed, and cut in half crosswise if beans are very long

9 ounces white boiling potatoes, peeled, halved lengthwise, and cut into ¼-inch slices (about 1 ¾ cups)

1 cup homemade pesto (either *Pesto Tradizionale* on page 66 or *Pesto nel Mixer* on page 67)

1 pound trenette or linguine

Finely grated Parmigiano-Reggiano, for serving

Serves 4 to 6

♦ In a large pot of generously salted, boiling water, cook green beans until tender but still al dente, 5 to 7 minutes. With a spider or slotted spoon, transfer beans to a colander. Return cooking water to a boil and add the potatoes. Cook until tender when poked with a fork, but not yet falling apart, 7 to 9 minutes. Using a spider or slotted spoon, transfer potatoes to colander with green beans.

Scoop the pesto into a large serving bowl.

Bring cooking water back to a boil, add pasta, and cook until al dente. Scoop out a cup of pasta cooking water in a heatproof measuring cup or mug. Drain the pasta in the colander, directly on top of the cooked vegetables. (This will warm up the vegetables if they have cooled off in the meantime.)

Stir a few tablespoons of pasta water into the pesto to thin it out slightly. (It should be smooth and creamy, like a thick bisque, but neither pasty nor soupy.) Add the pasta and cooked vegetables and toss to combine, adding more pasta water as necessary for desired consistency.

Serve hot with freshly grated Parmigiano-Reggiano cheese.

Ravioli di Carne con Tócco

Meat Ravioli with Tócco Sauce

½ pound mixed greens
  (such as escarole, borage, beet
  greens, and spinach)

Salt

1 slice stale or lightly toasted white
  sandwich bread, crusts removed

½ cup beef broth (or water)

Extra-virgin olive oil

½ medium yellow onion, diced

1 tablespoon pine nuts (optional),
  chopped

¼ pound pork sausage, casings
  removed

4 ounces of cooked beef
  (use the meat from *Tócco*, page 126,
  or a leftover pot roast) shredded,
  and finely minced (½ cup)

1 ounce finely grated Parmigiano-
  Reggiano (about ¼ cup, packed)

1 teaspoon minced marjoram

A pinch of freshly grated nutmeg

1 large egg, lightly beaten

1 recipe *Pasta Fresca Ligure*
  (page 60)

Tócco sauce (page 126)

Serves 6 to 8

Most of Liguria's stuffed pastas are filled with foraged greens, pumpkin, or other vegetables from the poor, agricultural hillsides. However, Genoa was once a powerful maritime empire, and families made rich on trade and war could afford the luxury of meat. There, you'll find many variations of meat-filled ravioli, although most contain greens as well. Meat ravioli are commonly dressed with *Tócco* sauce (page 126), and use the leftover meat in the filling.

♦ Wash the greens and boil in a large pot of generously salted water until tender, 2 to 3 minutes, then drain. When cool enough to handle, wring out excess moisture, transfer to a cutting board and finely chop; place in a large bowl and set aside. Place the bread slices in a wide, shallow dish, cover with beef broth, and set aside until absorbed, about 5 minutes.

Heat a tablespoon of olive oil in a large frying pan over medium heat and cook onion until translucent, about 5 minutes. Add pine nuts (if using), and sausage; continue to sauté until meat is browned and cooked through. Transfer the mixture onto a cutting board and finely chop. Add sausage mixture to the bowl with the greens, and add *Tócco* meat. Remove bread from broth and squeeze to release excess liquid. Finely crumble the bread and transfer to the bowl; discard broth. Add Parmigiano-Reggiano, marjoram, nutmeg, ¼ teaspoon salt, and egg; mix well.

Roll out 1 rectangular sheet of pasta as thinly as possible following the instructions on page 60. If desired, transfer the mixture to a pastry bag with a wide, round tip. Lay pasta sheet on a floured surface and distribute ½ teaspoon mounds of filling at regular intervals in a straight line along one lengthwise half of the sheet. The mounds should be 1 ½ to 2 inches apart, and at least ¾ of an inch from the edge of pasta. Moisten the other half of the dough with a pastry brush dipped in water. Carefully lift the pasta sheet and fold it over the filling. Press around the filling with your fingertips to seal and remove air pockets. Cut between each mound of filling with a knife or ravioli cutter. If necessary, press around the edges of the individual ravioli with your fingertips to seal completely. Trim each ravioli so that only a ⅛-inch border remains around the filling, making sure it's properly sealed, or they will fall apart while cooking. Transfer to a tray lined with a clean, flour-dusted kitchen towel; do not to let them overlap. Repeat with remaining pasta and filling.

Cook ravioli in a large pot of generously salted water until cooked through but still al dente, 6 to 9 minutes. Carefully transfer to a colander with a spider or slotted spoon. Serve immediately.

Ravioli di Magro

Meatless Ravioli

The first thing Nadia of Sestri Levante's innovative restaurant Cantine Cattaneo told me when we met was, *"La Liguria é il raviolo."* ("Liguria *is* ravioli.") At the time, I didn't think much about the assertion. I chalked it up to an obsession of her partner, chef Enrico Bo, who creates new, elaborate iterations of ravioli for every season and every new tasting menu. "It's like a blank canvas in the shape of Liguria," she insisted. After traveling extensively in the region and tasting more ravioli than one human probably should, I agree with Nadia: It is the food that best defines this part of the world.

Ravioli marry Ligurians' love for stuffed food with their passion for pasta and thrift; this miracle of a dish transforms humble ingredients into an elegant, substantial meal. There is a firm (though unproven) local belief that ravioli were invented in Genoa, and you will find countless variations and recipes across the region. Ubiquitous in the inland trattoria and pasta shops, *Ravioli di magro* are often served with a meat sauce like ragú or *Tócco* (recipe on page 126). Feel free to experiment with different fresh greens for the filling, but always use a mix to ensure a balanced flavor. You may also include *Preboggión* (see page 78) if you're in a foraging mood.

2 pounds mixed greens
  (such as escarole, borage, beet
  greens, arugula, and spinach)
Salt
2 slices stale or lightly toasted white
  sandwich bread, crusts removed
⅔ cup milk
Extra-virgin olive oil
1 medium yellow onion, diced
1 garlic clove, minced
2 large eggs
1 ½ ounces finely grated Parmigiano-
  Reggiano (about ½ cup, packed)
2 teaspoons minced marjoram
1 recipe *Pasta Fresca Ligure* (page 60)

Serves 6 to 8

◆ Bring a large pot of generously salted water to a boil. Wash the greens and cook until tender, about 5 minutes, then drain. When cool enough to handle, wring out excess moisture with your hands, transfer to a food processor, and process until finely chopped. Place the bread slices in a single layer in a wide, shallow dish, cover with milk, and set aside until bread has absorbed it, about 5 minutes.

Heat a tablespoon of olive oil in a small frying pan over medium heat and cook onion until translucent, about 5 minutes. Stir in garlic, cook for 1 minute, and then remove pan from heat. Transfer mixture to the food processor with the greens. Remove bread slices from milk and squeeze to release excess liquid, tear into pieces, and add to the food processor. Add the eggs; blend on medium speed until well combined. Add Parmigiano-Reggiano, 1 tablespoon olive oil, marjoram, and ¼ teaspoon salt. Pulse mixture until combined, about 30 seconds.

Continued...

Roll out 1 rectangular sheet of pasta as thinly as possible following the instructions on page 60. If desired, transfer the mixture to a pastry bag with a wide, round tip. Lay pasta sheet on a floured surface and distribute ½ teaspoon mounds of filling at regular intervals in a straight line along one lengthwise half of the sheet. The mounds should be 1 ½ to 2 inches apart, and at least ¾ of an inch from the edge of pasta. Moisten the other half of the dough with a pastry brush dipped in water. Carefully lift the pasta sheet and fold it over the filling. Press around the filling with your fingertips to seal and remove air pockets. Cut between each mound of filling with a knife or ravioli cutter. If necessary, press around the edges of the individual ravioli with your fingertips to seal completely. Trim each raviolo so that only a thin (⅛-inch) border remains around the filling, but make sure it's properly sealed, or they will fall apart while cooking. Transfer ravioli to a tray lined with a clean, flour-dusted kitchen towel, careful not to let them overlap, or they will stick together. Repeat with remaining pasta and filling.

Cook ravioli in a large pot of generously salted water until cooked through but still al dente, 4 to 6 minutes. Carefully transfer to a colander with a spider or slotted spoon. Serve hot with desired sauce or toss them gently with melted butter, fresh sage leaves, and finely grated Parmigiano-Reggiano.

Ravioli di Pesce

Fish Ravioli

Trattoria Raieü (which means *raviolo* in local dialect), is known for traditional cuisine and fresh fish, and for good reason. Lorenzo is the third generation to work in his family's restaurant, and the only one that followed his grandfather's footsteps as a fisherman. "In my *nonno's* time, fish was cheap. The lack of refrigeration meant you could sell the day's catch locally. So, my grandmother started making and selling ravioli and other traditional dishes with the leftovers to make ends meet...and here we are today." The lamps that illuminate the wooden booths of the restaurant were repurposed from his grandfather's original fishing boat.

This recipe is inspired by his historic restaurant's famous *Ravioli di Pesce*. You can use 1 ½ cups (9 ½ ounces) of any leftover, cooked white fish in the filling (for instance from *Branzino alla Ligure* on page 111). Remember never to serve any fish pasta dishes with Parmigiano, or any milk products. I pressed Lorenzo's aunt in the kitchen about this rule, and the only answer she offered was, "Everyone knows fish and dairy don't get along."

♦ Place the bread slices in a single layer in a wide, shallow dish, cover with fish broth or water, and set aside until bread has absorbed the liquid, about 5 minutes.

Rinse the fish inside and out and place in a wide, deep sauté pan. Cover with cold water and bring to a simmer over medium heat. Add 2 teaspoons of salt, adjust heat to keep water just below the boiling point until fish is tender and flakes away when poked with a sharp knife, 8 to 10 minutes. Transfer fish to a plate and set aside until cool enough to handle.

Clean the fish by removing and discarding the skin, head, and bones. Shred the meat with your fingers, carefully removing any pin bones hidden in the flesh. Finely chop the meat and transfer to a large bowl. Remove bread slices from broth and squeeze to release excess liquid, crumble finely and add to the bowl; discard broth. Add salt to taste, the egg, lemon zest, garlic, and parsley. Mix well.

Roll out 1 rectangular sheet of pasta as thinly as possible following the instructions on page 60. If desired, transfer the mixture to a pastry bag with a wide, round tip. Lay pasta sheet on a floured surface and distribute ½ teaspoon mounds of filling at regular intervals in a straight line along one lengthwise half of the sheet. The mounds should be 1 ½ to 2 inches apart, and at least ¾ of an inch from the edge of pasta. Moisten the other half of the dough with a pastry brush dipped in water. Carefully lift the pasta sheet and fold it over the filling. Press around the filling with your fingertips to seal and remove air pockets. Cut between each mound of filling with a knife or ravioli cutter. If

4 slices of stale or lightly toasted white sandwich bread, crusts removed

1 cup fish stock or water

1 whole, medium (18 ounces) sea bass or other, mild white fish, gutted and cleaned

Salt

1 large egg, lightly beaten

½ teaspoon finely grated lemon zest

¼ teaspoon finely minced garlic

2 teaspoons finely minced flat-leaf parsley

1 teaspoon finely minced marjoram

1 recipe *Pasta Fresca Ligure* (page 60)

Sugo per Ravioli di Pesce (facing page), light tomato sauce, or olive oil, for serving

Serves 4 to 6

necessary, press around the edges of the individual ravioli with your finger-tips to seal completely. Trim each raviolo so that only a thin (⅛-inch) border remains around the filling, but make sure it's properly sealed, or they will fall apart while cooking. Transfer ravioli to a tray lined with a clean, flour-dusted kitchen towel, careful not to let them overlap, or they will stick together. Repeat with remaining pasta and filling.

Cook ravioli in a large pot of generously salted water until cooked through but still al dente, 6 to 9 minutes. Carefully transfer to a colander with a spider or slotted spoon.

Serve with *Sugo per Ravioli di Pesce*, a light tomato sauce, or simply with olive oil (but no Parmigiano!).

Sugo per Ravioli di Pesce

Seafood Sauce for Fish Ravioli

5 plum tomatoes

Extra-virgin olive oil

1 clove of garlic, unpeeled

Salt

1 pound mussels, scrubbed and debearded

12 to 16 raw unpeeled red prawns or royal red shrimp, head-on (count 2 per person)

1 tablespoon finely chopped flat-leaf parsley

Serves 6 to 8

Bring a medium saucepan of water to boil over high heat. Score an X on the bottom of each tomato and blanch in boiling water for 2 minutes; drain and set aside until cool enough to handle. Peel tomatoes and cut in half lengthwise. Carefully remove as many seeds as possible without squeezing the tomatoes (this would release all the juices we want to conserve for the sauce). Don't obsess over this step, it's only important to get rid of a large part of the seeds, not every last one. Chop the tomato pulp into chunks.

Heat 2 tablespoons of olive oil in a large frying pan over medium-high heat. Add the unpeeled garlic clove and swirl to coat in oil. Add tomato pulp and a generous pinch of salt; stir to combine. Cover and simmer for 15 to 20 minutes. Add mussels, cover, and cook over high heat until the mussels open, about 5 minutes. Transfer mussels to a bowl using a slotted spoon; set aside and keep warm.

Meanwhile, clean the shrimp: leaving the heads attached, peel and de-vein the body and tail of each shrimp. Add the shrimp to the pan and stir to coat with sauce. Bring to a boil, then lower to a slow simmer, cover, and cook until shrimp are opaque, about 5 minutes. Transfer shrimp to a plate using a slotted spoon and keep warm. Add parsley and a tablespoon of extra-virgin olive oil to the sauce. Remove garlic clove and add salt to taste.

Cook the ravioli according to the instructions in the recipe. When ready, transfer the cooked ravioli to the pan with the warm sauce and stir gently to combine. Divide ravioli between warmed serving plates, top with mussels and shrimp and serve immediately.

Preboggión

While leafing through antique Ligurian cookbooks loaned to me by Genovese friends and family, I was immediately intrigued by the omnipresence of one mysterious ingredient. Preboggión, or prebuggiún, is a mix of foraged herbs and greens from forests and mountain pastures, used in soups, ravioli, rice, omelets, savory pies, and more. I've been told the mix can contain up to thirty-two different edible wild herbs, but most local foragers I've pressed have only named around ten of the most common. Depending on what is available locally, borage, wild chicory, thistle, lovage, dandelion, bristly hawkbit, chard, sorrel, rapunzel, chervil, wild fennel, maidenstears, and poppy leaves all find their way into the mix. The herbs are carefully washed and blanched in salted, boiling water for 10-30 seconds before being used in the various recipes.

Chef Paolo Cagnoli of *Villa Argentina* in Moneglia entrusts a local forager with the job of collecting basketfuls of these wild herbs between May and September, which he integrates into his menu regularly. He recommends shocking the prebuggiún in an ice bath immediately after blanching to preserve its brilliant green color. After draining it thoroughly, Paolo blends the mixture until smooth, filters it through a fine-mesh sieve and then uses it as a pasta sauce or to flavor soups and risottos. Paolo told me there is an art to mixing prebuggiún that only experience can provide. "Each plant has a specific flavor," he explained, "so the mix must be balanced to avoid one flavor overwhelming the others."

If you have the opportunity to forage yourself, I encourage you to seek out some of the above herbs. If the only foraging in your future is at the grocery store, you can easily fake a prebuggiún with a store-bought mix of spring greens, swiss chard, borage, parsley, lettuce, spinach, escarole, and endive. Blanch and shock the greens as indicated above before proceeding with the desired recipe.

Pansoti

"Paunchy" Pasta Filled with Foraged Greens

The name *pansoti* is derived from the local dialect term for "belly," in reference to the ravioli's pudgy appearance. For this recipe, one of Liguria's most delicious and iconic, I turned to Enrica Monzani, a Genoa-based food blogger, for help. She explained that they are traditionally stuffed with the elusive mix of foraged herbs and greens known as *Preboggión* (page 78) and the fresh local cheese *prescinsêua*: ingredients hard to come by outside the region, but commonly substituted with mixed greens and ricotta. Serve *pansoti* with *Salsa di Noci* (page 83) or simply with melted butter and freshly grated Parmigiano-Reggiano.

♦ Wash the greens and boil in a large pot of generously salted water until tender, about 5 minutes; drain. When cool enough to handle, wring out excess moisture, and chop finely, removing any thick stems that remained overly tough. Heat a tablespoon of olive oil in a small frying pan over medium heat and add whole garlic clove, stir for 1 minute, then add chopped greens. Sauté for 2 to 3 minutes until any remaining liquid has evaporated and greens are shiny and garlic-scented. Transfer greens to a large bowl and let cool for 5 minutes; discard garlic. Add the egg, *prescinsêua*, Parmigiano-Reggiano, minced marjoram, nutmeg, salt, and pepper. Stir to combine.

Cut 1 fist-sized portion of dough and roll out following the instructions on page 60. If using a pasta machine, roll to the second-to-thinnest setting. Lay pasta sheet on a floured surface and cut into 3-inch squares. Drop a teaspoon of filling in the center of each square (I like to transfer the filling to a pastry bag with a wide, round tip to help with this step). Lightly brush the sides of the pasta with water and fold the dough diagonally over the filling to form a triangle. Press along the edges with your fingertips to seal. Join together the two diagonal corners of the triangle and press with your fingers to seal them together. Transfer shaped *pansoti* to a tray lined with a clean, flour-dusted kitchen towel or parchment, careful not to let them overlap, or they will stick together. Repeat with remaining pasta and filling.

Bring a large pot of generously salted water to a rolling boil and add a tablespoon of olive oil. Transfer the walnut sauce to a medium bowl; set aside. Carefully lower *pansoti* into boiling water and gently simmer until cooked through but still al dente, 7 to 9 minutes. If serving with walnut sauce, dilute the sauce with ¼ to ½ cup of the cooking water and stir until creamy. Carefully transfer cooked *pansoti* to individual serving plates or a wide shallow bowl with a spider or slotted spoon. Drizzle lightly with oil, gently toss to coat, then pour the walnut sauce over the pasta. Serve immediately.

2 pounds 4 ounces mixed
  Preboggión (see page 78) or a mix
  of fresh greens (Swiss chard, spinach,
  borage, escarole, and endive)
1 clove of garlic
Extra-virgin olive oil
1 large egg
½ cup (4.25 ounces) *prescinsêua* or
  ⅓ cup ricotta cheese plus 3
  tablespoons Greek yogurt
1 ounce finely grated
  Parmigiano-Reggiano cheese
  (about ¼ cup, packed)
1 tablespoon fresh marjoram,
  finely chopped
⅛ teaspoon freshly grated nutmeg
½ teaspoon salt
¼ teaspoon freshly ground black pepper
1 recipe *Pasta for Pansoti*
  (recipe on page 82)
1 recipe *Salsa di Noci*
  (recipe on page 83)

Serves 6 to 8

Pasta per Pansoti

Pasta for Pansoti

The pasta for *pansoti* is traditionally made without eggs, only flour, water, and white wine. I suffered through several frustrating trials with the resulting dough: overly-elastic, sticky, and impossible to shape into ravioli. Each time I ended up scrapping the whole mess and making an egg dough instead, which is endlessly more manageable. Discouraged, I turned to my friend Paolo Cagnoli, chef at *Villa Argentina* in Moneglia, for help. I was sure there was some trick to it, some secret technique that Ligurian chefs and grandmothers use to shape the impossible pasta.

"Of course there is a trick, Laurel," he replied softly with his typical sly grin, "It's that everyone slips at least one egg in the dough, whether they admit it or not."

♦   Pour the flour in a mound in the center of a large work surface. Make a well in the center and crack the eggs into it. Add wine and water to eggs and stir with a fork, without incorporating the flour, until yolks and whites are blended. Begin incorporating bits of the flour from the walls of the well with your fingertips. Continue to work in more flour until it is all combined and a shaggy, sticky mass has formed. You may add more water, 1 tablespoon at a time, if dough isn't coming together. Begin kneading and folding with your hands until the dough becomes satiny and elastic, about 10 minutes (you may also use a bench scraper to help with this process). If the dough is still sticky after 10 minutes, sprinkle with a bit more flour and continue kneading until smooth. Alternatively, you may combine flour, eggs, and water in a food processor. Process for 30 to 60 seconds. If the dough doesn't come together, add another teaspoon of water and process again. Repeat as necessary until dough comes together in a rough, shaggy ball. Remove the dough from the food processor and transfer to a clean work surface. Knead by hand for a minute or two until it comes together into a smooth ball. The dough is ready when it springs back after being poked with a fingertip. Form into a ball, wrap tightly with plastic wrap, and let rest at room temperature for 30 minutes to 1 hour.

4 cups (18 ounces) all-purpose flour

2 large eggs

¼ cup dry white wine

½ cup plus 2 tablespoons room temperature water

Serves 6 to 8

Salsa di Noci

Walnut Sauce

2 slices stale or lightly toasted white
  sandwich bread, crusts removed
⅔ cup milk
2 cups (7 ounces) walnut halves
  or pieces
½ clove of garlic, peeled
½ teaspoon minced marjoram
1 ounce finely grated Parmigiano-
  Reggiano (about ¼ cup, packed)
Salt
5 tablespoons mild-flavored
  extra-virgin olive oil

Serves 6 to 8

While this creamy walnut sauce is most often served with *pansoti* (recipe on page 81), it can also be used to dress your pasta of choice. Don't be tempted to add any actual cream as some local restaurants have begun doing in recent years; it makes the sauce cloying and heavy, and overpowers the rich, earthy flavor of the nuts. Remember to reserve some pasta cooking water to dilute the thick sauce before serving. If desired, you may garnish the finished pasta dish with diced walnuts and marjoram leaves.

♦ Place the bread slices in a single layer in a wide, shallow dish, cover with milk, and set aside until bread has absorbed it, about 5 minutes. Remove bread slices from milk, squeeze to wring out excess liquid, and place in the bowl of a food processor or blender. Add walnuts, garlic, marjoram, Parmigiano-Reggiano, and ¼ teaspoon salt. Blend until the walnuts are finely ground. With the machine running on low speed, begin adding the olive oil through the feeder tube, 1 tablespoon at a time, stopping occasionally to scrape down the sides of the bowl. After all the oil has been added, add 2 to 3 tablespoons of lukewarm water while blending on medium speed, until the mixture is thick, smooth, and well blended. Before serving, add some pasta cooking water to thin out the sauce to desired consistency.

Turle

Potato, Cheese, and Mint Ravioli

In a relatively unknown corner of Liguria, hidden high in the foothills of the Maritime Alps, lies a cluster of villages bound by what they have dubbed as their unique culinary patrimony: *cucina bianca* or "white cuisine." Here we are hiking distance from both the French border and neighboring Piedmont, and though we're a mere twenty miles from the beach, the food looks nothing like Mediterranean cuisine. These mountain folk and shepherds rely on hearty dishes, heavy on dairy and "white" winter vegetables: leeks, potatoes, cabbages, turnips, garlic, and seasoned with the fresh foraged herbs of mountain pastures. Of course, this is still Liguria, so you will always find some sort of stuffed pasta on the menu, like these irresistible potato, cheese, and mint ravioli, a perfect example of the elusive *cucina bianca*.

♦ Place potatoes in a wide pot and cover with cold water. Add 3 tablespoons salt and bring to a boil over high heat. Lower heat and simmer until potatoes are tender all the way through when poked with a sharp knife, from 10 to 20 minutes, depending on the size. Remove potatoes from water with a spider or slotted spoon as they are ready and set aside until just cool enough to handle but still hot. Peel potatoes, break into chunks, and feed through a potato ricer into a large bowl. Alternatively, mash with a fork or potato masher. While potatoes are still warm, add Toma, Parmigiano-Reggiano, and egg yolks. Finely dice half of the mint leaves and add to the mixture. Stir until well combined. Add a pinch of salt and a few grinds of black pepper; set aside.

Roll out 1 rectangular sheet of pasta as thinly as possible following the instructions on page 60. Using a 2 ½-inch round cookie cutter or a small glass, cut out as many rounds of dough as possible. Drop ½ teaspoon of filling in the center of each round, moisten the edges with a pastry brush or finger dipped in water, then fold the dough in half over the filling, creating a half-moon shape. Press around the filling with your fingertips to seal and remove air pockets. If desired, crimp around the edges with the tines of a fork for a decorative finish. Transfer ravioli to a tray lined with a clean, flour-dusted kitchen towel, careful not to let them overlap, or they will stick together. Repeat with remaining pasta and filling.

Cook *turle* in a large pot of generously salted water until cooked through but still al dente, 5 to 7 minutes. Meanwhile, melt butter in a large frying pan over medium heat; when butter is melted and frothy, remove from heat and add remaining mint leaves. Carefully transfer the ravioli to a large serving dish using a spider or slotted spoon. Drizzle with melted butter and serve hot with pepper and Parmigiano-Reggiano.

1 pound whole russet potatoes, scrubbed

3 tablespoons salt, plus more as needed

About 1 cup (5 ounces) diced or grated Toma cheese (you may substitute with a mild brie or fresh Asiago)

2 ½ ounces finely grated Parmigiano-Reggiano (about ¾ cup, packed), plus more for serving

2 large egg yolks

10 fresh mint leaves

1 recipe *Pasta Fresca Ligure* (recipe on page 60)

½ cup unsalted butter

Salt and freshly ground black pepper to taste

Serves 6 to 8

Gnocchi di Castagne

Chestnut Flour Gnocchi

Chestnuts appear frequently in Ligurian cuisine: from the extravagant candied chestnuts of Genoa's pastry shops to omnipresent homemade pastas, rustic breads, and cakes. While Liguria's steep, woodland hillsides proved problematic for growing wheat, her forests abounded with chestnuts, which played an integral role in local commerce.

I first tried this dish at one of my favorite Ligurian restaurants, La Brinca, and was charmed by the hearty chew and earthy flavor of the gnocchi, beautifully paired with fresh basil pesto (La Brinca is one of the few establishments that still painstakingly makes their pesto with a mortar and pestle), or simply with melted butter and fresh sage leaves. If you like, you can gently roll each *gnocco* down the tines of a fork to make the characteristic grooves, but it's not required, and skipping this step will save you loads of time.

♦ Place potatoes in a wide pot, cover with cold water, add 3 tablespoons salt, and bring to a boil over high heat. Lower heat and simmer until potatoes are tender all the way through when poked with a sharp knife, from 10 to 20 minutes, depending on the size. Remove potatoes from water with a slotted spoon as they are ready and set aside until just cool enough to handle.

Peel potatoes, break into chunks, and feed through a potato ricer onto a clean work surface. Alternatively, mash in a large bowl with a fork or potato masher, then pour onto a clean work surface. Sift flours together over the mashed potatoes, sprinkle with ½ teaspoon salt, and drizzle with olive oil. Push and fold the mixture using your hands or a bench scraper until a shaggy mass forms. Knead on a flour-dusted surface until dough is soft and pliable, and all the flour is incorporated. Do not overmix, or the gnocchi will be tough.

Line 2 rimmed baking trays with parchment paper and sprinkle with flour; set aside. Break off a handful of dough (cover remaining dough with a kitchen towel so it doesn't dry out) and roll into a log about ¾-inch thick. Cut the log crosswise at 1-inch intervals to make rectangular gnocchi. If you like, you can gently roll each *gnocco* down the tines of a fork to make the characteristic grooves; otherwise, leave them as they are. Transfer the finished gnocchi to a parchment-lined tray, being careful not to overlap or let them touch each other, or they will stick. Repeat with remaining dough. Sprinkle the tops of the gnocchi with a bit of flour.

Cook the gnocchi in batches in a large pot of generously salted boiling water. The gnocchi are ready a few seconds after they float to the surface of the water. Gently transfer them to a large bowl with a spider or slotted spoon. Serve immediately with pesto or melted butter and sage leaves.

2 pounds russet potatoes, scrubbed

3 tablespoons plus ½ teaspoon salt, divided

2 cups (9 ounces) chestnut flour

½ cup (2 ¼ ounces) all-purpose flour, plus more for dusting

2 tablespoons extra-virgin olive oil

1 cup homemade pesto
(either *Pesto Tradizionale* on page 66 or *Pesto nel Mixer* on page 67), or butter and fresh sage leaves, for serving

Serves 4 to 6

Lattughe Ripiene

Stuffed Lettuce Packets in Broth

One of the more elegant manifestations of the Ligurian penchant for stuffing food, this sophisticated dish, traditionally served at Easter, harkens back to the haute bourgeoisie of 1700s Genoa, the only ones at the time who could afford the luxury of meat. A flavorful veal and pork filling is sealed inside blanched lettuce leaves, and then simmered in a homemade veal or beef broth. (For a vegetarian version, substitute one pound diced, fresh mushrooms and a half of a pound finely chopped eggplant for the meat. Sauté with onion until tender and swap a homemade vegetable stock for the meat broth.) You may also simmer the assembled rolls (vegetarian or not) in a simple tomato sauce instead of broth for a popular variation on this classic.

20 to 24 large, outer leaves from about 3 heads of butter or Bibb lettuce

2 tablespoons unsalted butter

1 yellow onion, finely diced

½ pound ground veal

½ pound ground pork

1 clove of garlic, finely chopped

Salt

1 ½ ounces finely grated Parmigiano-Reggiano (about ½ cup, packed), plus more for serving

2 large eggs, lightly beaten

2 tablespoons minced flat-leaf parsley

1 teaspoon minced marjoram leaves

⅓ cup plain breadcrumbs

5 cups homemade veal or light beef broth, hot

Serves 4 to 6

♦ Bring a large pot of generously salted water to a boil over high heat. Prepare a large bowl of ice water. Quickly blanch lettuce leaves in the boiling water, in batches as necessary, until just softened, 1 to 3 seconds. Immediately transfer leaves to ice bath with a spider or slotted spoon and cool completely. Drain carefully and spread out leaves to dry flat on a couple of clean kitchen towels.

Melt butter in a large frying pan over medium-high heat. Add onion and cook until translucent, about 5 minutes. Add ground meat, raise heat to high and sauté until browned and fragrant. Stir in garlic and continue to cook for 30 seconds, then remove from heat. Transfer mixture to a large bowl and let cool slightly. Add a generous pinch of salt, the Parmigiano-Reggiano, eggs, parsley, marjoram, and breadcrumbs, and stir to combine.

Spread a lettuce leaf flat on a clean cutting board and drop 1 to 2 tablespoons of filling in the center. Fold the two sides over the filling and then roll the leaf up like a little burrito. The leaf should stick to itself and remain closed, but you may tie it with a piece of kitchen twine if it looks like it wants to pop open. Place rolls, folded side down, in a skillet or saucepan, making sure they fit snugly (this will help keep them intact). Gently pour in broth, just enough to cover rolls, and bring to a slow simmer over medium heat. Cook gently for 6 to 7 minutes. Carefully pour most of the broth out of the pan and into a bowl or pitcher, making sure the lettuce rolls don't fall out. Very gently remove the lettuce rolls from the pan, one at a time, and divide them between individual bowls, placing 4 rolls in each bowl. Ladle hot broth over rolls in each bowl and serve immediately, topped with freshly grated Parmigiano-Reggiano.

Minestrone alla Genovese

Genovese Minestrone

3 ½ ounces fresh borlotti beans
   (or substitute with ½ cup canned
   kidney beans, drained and rinsed)
2 medium zucchini, chopped into small
   cubes
1 cup (3 ½ ounces) fresh, coarsely
   chopped green beans
2 carrots, chopped
½ cup fresh, shelled peas
   (or substitute with frozen peas)
1 cup diced savoy cabbage
1 celery stalk, chopped
1 cup chard or spinach chopped
1 large leek, white and light green
   parts only, diced
1 small eggplant (or half of a large
   eggplant), chopped into small cubes
2 medium boiling potatoes, peeled
   and chopped into small cubes
¾ cup chopped butternut, acorn,
   or other squash
1 teaspoon salt
1 rind of a wedge of Parmigiano-
   Reggiano cheese
3 ½ ounces of small, short pasta,
   like tubetti or ditalini
¼ cup pesto, with or without pine nuts
   (recipe on page 66 or 67)

Serves 6 to 8

This thick vegetable stew, swirled with fresh pesto before serving, is a Genovese classic. While you might imagine minestrone as a warming winter soup, in Liguria, it is traditionally a summer dish that takes advantage of the abundant garden produce the season provides. Like pesto, this is one of those hotly contested family recipes passed down for generations; everyone thinks their *nonna* knew best, and no one agrees on the exact ingredients or procedure. My friend Rosa's cousin, for example, refuses to give her their grandmother's recipe because Rosa doesn't have a marble sink, which the cousin argues is fundamental for the correct execution of the dish. Traditionalists insist you make pesto sans-pine nuts for the soup, but my mother-in-law says it's better with, so I'll leave it up to you. Personally, I never argue with my mother-in-law.

Make sure to save the rind of your Parmigiano-Reggiano after you've grated away all the cheese. I freeze them so I always have one on hand to add a flavorful umami kick to broths and soups.

Only cook the pasta directly in the pot of soup if you'll be serving it immediately; otherwise, it will turn to mush. Alternatively, you may cook the pasta separately in generously salted water until al dente, drain, rinse under cold water, toss with a tablespoon of extra-virgin olive oil, and add to the soup when ready to serve.

◆ Combine the fresh beans and all the vegetables in a large soup pot (if using canned beans, you will add them later). Cover with cold water (the water should come about 1 inch above the veggies). Bring to a rolling boil over high heat, add salt, then lower to a simmer and cook, covered, for 30 minutes, stirring occasionally. Add the rind of Parmigiano-Reggiano (if you are using canned beans, you may add them at this point). Continue to simmer, adding a splash of water occasionally if necessary, until vegetables are so soft they break apart easily with a spoon, about 2 hours total. Taste, and add more salt if necessary. Add pasta to soup, cook until still very al dente; remove from heat. Alternatively, you may cook the pasta separately in generously salted water until al dente, drain, rinse under cold water, toss with a tablespoon of extra virgin olive oil, and add to the soup just before you're ready to serve it. Stir in pesto and let rest for 15 minutes before serving the soup with olive oil and freshly grated Parmigiano-Reggiano.

Risotto Lavanda e Rosmarino

Lavender and Rosemary Risotto

While lavender farming is most often associated with the iconic purple fields of Provence, France, the Italian Riviera has a long history of cultivating and distilling the aromatic herb since Roman times. This thriving industry was almost completely wiped out after cheaper, artificial lavender scents came on the market in the 1960s. Fortunately, it has been enjoying a revival in recent years, mostly thanks to Lavanda Riviera dei Fiori, a nonprofit that brings together local farmers and chefs to promote Ligurian lavender, especially for culinary use. This recipe, shared with me by Lavanda Riviera dei Fiori's generous volunteers, beautifully pairs the flavors and aromas of western Liguria's Flower Riviera.

♦ Bring the broth to a simmer in a saucepan over medium-high heat; lower flame to maintain a slow simmer. Heat 2 tablespoons olive oil in a heavy, wide saucepan over medium heat. When oil is hot, add shallots and sauté, stirring constantly, until translucent but not yet golden.

Add the rice, rosemary, and lavender; cook, stirring constantly, until rice is hot to the touch and no longer opaque, 3 to 4 minutes. Add the wine and stir until it has absorbed, about 3 minutes. Stir in a ladleful of broth and cook, stirring often, until broth is mostly absorbed, 2 to 3 minutes. Continue to add the broth, one or two ladlesful at a time, stirring until absorbed. Try to keep rice submerged under a thin layer of broth at all times (this is to ensure all the grains cook evenly). Adjust heat to between medium and medium-low to keep the risotto barely simmering. Cook, stirring often, until rice is just tender but still al dente (not mushy). The risotto should have the consistency of a creamy porridge and move in slow waves when you shake the pan, but it should not be soupy. Remove from heat, add remaining 3 tablespoons olive oil, Parmigiano-Reggiano, lemon zest, and juice; stir until creamy and well combined.

Divide between individual warm plates, decorate with fresh lavender flowers, and serve immediately with freshly grated Parmigiano-Reggiano.

5 to 7 cups low-sodium light beef, chicken, or vegetable broth

5 tablespoons extra-virgin olive oil, divided

2 shallots, peeled and diced

2 cups carnaroli rice

2 teaspoons minced rosemary

1 teaspoon minced, dried lavender

½ cup dry white wine

1 ½ ounces finely grated Parmigiano-Reggiano (about ½ cup, packed)

1 teaspoon finely grated lemon zest

1 teaspoon fresh lemon juice

1 tablespoon fresh lavender flowers

Serves 4 to 6

Risotto con Erbe Aromatiche e Olive

Fresh Herb and Olive Risotto

While risotto comes from nearby Lombardy, the region surrounding Milan, today it is fully embraced by Liguria as well. Historically, soups, ravioli, and pasta were preferred to rice as a first course in this area, but today home cooks and professional chefs alike love to dress up Italy's favorite rice dish with local Ligurian flavors.

Zia Marghe, our family's matriarch, often makes a huge pot of this summertime favorite at our family home in Moneglia. In August, twenty or more of us regularly gather around the long marble table overlooking the Mediterranean sunset after a long day at the beach. Zia Marghe loves this recipe because, even when the refrigerator is empty, we always have a jar of olives and a garden full of fresh herbs for throwing together this fragrant risotto.

2 shallots, peeled and diced

1 tablespoon chopped rosemary leaves

1 tablespoon chopped thyme leaves

1 tablespoon chopped marjoram leaves

1 teaspoon chopped sage leaves

½ cup pitted green olives, such as Cerignola or Manzanilla

5 to 7 cups low-sodium chicken, beef, or vegetable broth

5 tablespoons extra-virgin olive oil

2 cups carnaroli or arborio rice

½ cup dry white wine

1 ½ ounces Parmigiano-Reggiano cheese (about ½ cup, packed), finely grated, plus more for serving

Serves 4 to 6

♦ Combine shallots, herbs, and olives in a food processor and pulse until minced and well combined. Bring the broth to a simmer in a saucepan over medium-high heat; lower flame to maintain a slow simmer. Heat 2 tablespoons of olive oil in a heavy, wide saucepan over medium heat. Add the rice and cook, stirring constantly, until rice is hot to the touch and no longer opaque, 3 to 4 minutes. Add the herb-olive mixture, and stir until fragrant, about 2 minutes. Pour in the wine and cook, stirring until it has absorbed, about 3 minutes. Stir in a ladleful of warm broth and cook, stirring often, until broth is mostly absorbed, 2 to 3 minutes. Continue to add the broth, one or two ladlesful at a time, stirring until absorbed. Try to keep rice submerged under a thin layer of broth at all times (this is to ensure all the grains of rice cook evenly). Adjust heat to between medium and medium-low to keep the risotto barely simmering. Cook, stirring often, until rice is just tender but still al dente (not mushy). The risotto should have the consistency of a creamy porridge and move in slow waves when you shake the pan, but it should not be soupy. Remove from heat, add remaining 3 tablespoons olive oil, the Parmigiano-Reggiano, and salt to taste; stir until creamy and well combined.

Divide between individual warm plates and serve immediately with freshly grated Parmigiano-Reggiano.

Pesce

◆

Fish

It is easy to assume that a region that stretches over 200 miles of coastline would rely heavily on seafood as its primary source of protein, but the truth about Liguria's relationship with seafood is complex and obscure. The Genovese, in the city's heyday, were merchants and sailors rather than fishermen. Today, while tourists flock to the beach towns in search of *pasta alle vongole* (pasta with clams) and *anelli fritti* (fried calamari), locals head for the hills to eat *Coniglio alla Ligure* (rabbit, page 125) — a primarily land-based cuisine. The sea in Liguria is not friendly to fishermen: Fish are scarce and waters are deep. Ligurians historically eyed the sea with mistrust, perhaps because of deep ancestral memories of losing loved ones to the swirling depths. Today's fishermen face different challenges. I talked to Massimo the fisherman as he docked his small fishing boat in the port in Camogli with the day's catch, as he has done most days, rain or shine, for the last thirty years. "There are no more fish in the sea," he lamented. "Climate change and pollution have changed everything."

This isn't to say that seafood is not part of Liguria's culinary patrimony. There are plenty of solid, traditional recipes for fish, with a predominance of *pesci azzurri* (literally "blue fish") a category which includes silver-skinned, oily fish, like anchovies, mackerel, sardines, and tuna. (Read more about Liguria's love affair with anchovies, and how to clean them, on page 104.) In this chapter I've highlighted some of the classic seafood dishes of Liguria, but avoided the more touristic offerings, which have only shown up in local restaurants in recent years.

Totani Ripieni

Stuffed Squid

6 medium squid with the tentacles,
  cleaned

3 slices of stale or lightly toasted white
  bread, crusts removed

½ cup milk

1 teaspoon finely chopped flat-leaf
  parsley

1 teaspoon diced marjoram

3 cloves of garlic, 2 minced and
  1 unpeeled

1 large egg

2 tablespoons pine nuts

1 ounce finely grated Parmigiano-
  Reggiano (about ¼ cup, packed)

Salt

2 tablespoons extra-virgin olive oil

½ cup dry white wine

1 14-ounce can crushed tomatoes

Serves 4 to 6

I can only imagine the delight of the first Ligurian cooks to get their hands on squid. Remember, this is a region obsessed with filling and stuffing even the most improbable foods (see *Lattughe Ripiene*, page 89), and when cleaned, squid becomes a natural pocket just begging to be filled. If you think you don't like squid, I urge you to try this recipe; it's certain to change your mind. You can ask your fishmonger to clean the squid for you if you're squeamish, but remember to request the tentacles; you will need them for the filling.

♦   Rinse the squid and pat dry; set aside. Place the bread in a wide, shallow dish and add the milk; set aside.

Finely chop the squid tentacles and place in a medium bowl. Add parsley, marjoram, the minced garlic, eggs, pine nuts, Parmigiano-Reggiano, ¼ teaspoon salt, and 1 tablespoon of olive oil. Remove the bread slices from the milk and squeeze to remove excess liquid. Break apart with your hands and add them to the bowl with the other ingredients. Mix well.

Spoon filling into the cavity of each squid, dividing it evenly among them. Be careful not to fill each one more than ¾ of the way full, as it will expand while cooking. Close the end of each squid by threading a toothpick through the open side.

Heat remaining tablespoon of olive oil in a wide saucepan or deep, straight-sided skillet over medium-high heat. Add the unpeeled clove of garlic and swirl to coat with oil. Carefully add the stuffed squid and cook, gently turning the squid once, until golden brown on both sides, 5 to 7 minutes. Add the wine and swirl the pan until it has evaporated, then add the crushed tomatoes and ¼ teaspoon salt. Bring to a simmer, cover, and cook over low heat until tomatoes have broken down into a sauce and squid is easily punctured with a fork, 35 to 40 minutes. Divide tomato sauce among plates, and place 1 stuffed squid on top. Serve while hot.

Ciuppin

Ligurian Fish Bisque

Extra-virgin olive oil

1 large yellow onion, finely diced

1 celery stalk, diced

1 large carrot, diced

4 cloves of garlic, minced

½ cup of dry white wine

4 plum tomatoes, chopped

4 pounds assorted whole,
  cleaned fish, heads and bones
  intact (see note), chopped
  into large sections

1 tablespoon tomato paste

Toasted slices of baguette
  or country bread

1 tablespoon chopped flat-leaf parsley

Special equipment:
Food mill

Serves 4 to 6

Ligurian sailors carried this ancient recipe far and wide, from their small fishing villages all the way to the docks of San Francisco, where it evolved into the more extravagant Italian-American seafood soup known as *cioppino*. It was born as a simple, frugal fisherman's stew, putting to use the bony fish and leftover scraps of the day's catch that didn't sell at market. The fish is simmered slowly with aromatics, then forced through a food mill (heads, bones, and all), filtered with a sieve, and served over stale bread. The result is a velvety, rich (albeit not very pretty) soup with complex flavor and pleasant texture. Today, many local restaurants gussy up the soup with chunks of fish, mussels, and shrimp to add a bit of flair in a preparation more closely resembling *cioppino*, but I prefer the fisherman's version you'll find below, elegant in its simplicity.

Note: Seek out a variety of fish such as red snapper, rockfish, red scorpionfish, red or grey mullet, monkfish, sea bream, John Dory, turbot, and gurnard. Shrimp and other crustaceans are also a nice touch but need to be peeled before adding to the soup. Avoid mackerel, herring, salmon, sardines, and other strongly flavored, oily fish.

♦ Coat the bottom of a large, heavy-bottomed pot generously with olive oil (about 2 tablespoons) and place over medium heat. Add onion, celery, and carrot, and cook until onion is translucent, about 5 minutes. Stir in garlic and cook for 1 minute; add wine and continue to cook, stirring until wine has almost completely evaporated. Add tomato pieces, cover, and cook over low heat for 15 minutes.

Add fish pieces and tomato paste, and cover with 4 cups of cold water. Bring to a boil over medium-high heat, lower to a simmer, and cook until fish completely falls apart, 45 minutes to 1 hour.

Working in batches, press soup through food mill into a clean pot (crush and break larger skeletons and bones with your hands before feeding through the food mill). Filter the soup with a sieve and heat over medium until hot. If the soup is too runny, boil until reduced to desired consistency; if too thick add a bit of water. Add salt and pepper to taste. Divide toasted bread among bowls, pour soup over the bread and garnish with parsley.

Acciughe Fritte a Cotoletta

Cutlet-style Fried Anchovies

The tiny, hectic kitchen at La Secca, the beach club our family frequents in Moneglia, churns out magnificently fresh seafood dishes from June through September before shuttering for the winter months. Salty-haired, barefoot children trot through the open-air veranda, gelato or granita in hand, dodging adults draped in sarongs and impressive tans, who impatiently await a free table. Once seated, carafes of lightly sparkling, white house wine flow freely, and the table soon overflows with *Zuppa di Muscoli* (Mussels Soup, page 108), *Calamari Ripieni* (Stuffed Squid, page 101) and *anelli fritti* (fried calamari). And of course, you can't miss the La Secca classic: *Acciughe fritte a cotoletta*, fresh anchovy filets dipped in egg, pressed in breadcrumbs, and fried until golden. Wherever I am in the world, one bite of this recipe and I'm transported straight to that breezy beachside veranda, with its blue and white striped awning, the lifeguard whistling in the distance, the blinding summer sunlight, and the briny sea air.

24 whole, fresh anchovies

2 large eggs

1 ½ cups plain breadcrumbs

Vegetable or grapeseed oil,
   for frying

Salt

Flat-leaf parsley, for garnishing

Lemon wedges, for serving

Serves 6

♦ Clean the anchovies, keeping the tail intact and opening them like a book (see instructions on page 104). Crack the eggs in a shallow bowl and beat lightly with a fork to combine. Pour the breadcrumbs into another shallow dish. Dip anchovies, one at a time, in the egg. Shake off excess then cover in breadcrumbs, pressing to adhere.

Heat about ½ an inch of oil in a wide, straight-sided frying pan over high heat until a pinch of breadcrumbs sizzles immediately and floats to the surface when it touches the oil. Fry the anchovies in batches, turning once, until golden and crunchy on both sides, about 5 minutes. Heat more oil between batches if necessary. Transfer cooked fish to a paper towel-lined plate and sprinkle with salt. Garnish with parsley and serve immediately with lemon wedges.

Acciughe

Anchovies

Fried, stuffed, stewed, marinated, baked, cured, or boiled, one could easily write an entire cookbook dedicated to Ligurian anchovy recipes. There is no other fish more emblematic of this region's cuisine. Small, cheap, and nutritious, there is nothing not to love about the tiny silver fish, and I'm not referring to that sad, salty, brown paste you find in typical Caesar salads. Buy whole anchovies fresh and follow the instructions below to clean them before using the fresh fillets in the recipe of your choice.

After many experiments, I've discovered the easiest way to clean anchovies is by hand; you don't even need a knife. First, prepare a clean cutting board where you will lay out the fillets. (I recommend using food-safe gloves for cleaning, otherwise, your hands will smell like anchovies for days.) Pinch the head of one anchovy between your thumb and forefinger and twist it away from the body. The head will easily detach, bringing most of the innards with it. Discard the head and guts. Slide the tip of your thumb along the fish's belly, carefully opening it; rinse out remaining innards. Gently pull out the central spine, starting from the side closest to the head of the fish, and flatten the fillet into a butterfly. Rinse the butterfly fillet and place on the prepared cutting board. Repeat with remaining fish. Fillets are now ready to marinate (recipe on page 46), stuff (recipe on page 107), or fry (recipe on page 103).

Acciughe Ripiene

Stuffed Anchovies

5 slices white sandwich bread, crusts
   removed

1 cup milk

46 whole, fresh anchovies
   (about 2 pounds)

2 tablespoons finely grated
   Parmigiano-Reggiano cheese

2 large eggs, lightly beaten with
   a fork

2 teaspoons finely chopped flat-leaf
   parsley

1 teaspoon finely chopped marjoram

1 clove garlic, minced

Salt and freshly ground black pepper

3 tablespoons plain breadcrumbs,
   plus more as necessary

Extra-virgin olive oil

Lemon wedges, for serving

Serves 6
   (makes 18 canapés, 3 per serving)

In our family, Zia Marghe is considered the queen of anchovies. I have a vivid memory of her and her husband, Zio Michi, bringing home an entire, twenty-pound case of the fresh fish, which they proceeded to clean in one sitting with admirable speed and dexterity. They carefully preserved most of the fish under salt in large buckets, to be enjoyed for the entire year to come. The fresh fillets that didn't end up under salt were stuffed with a flavorful mix of herbs, diced anchovies, and Parmigiano-Reggiano, and transformed into these sophisticated little silver "sandwiches," perfect as an elegant appetizer or eye-catching main course.

♦ Preheat the oven to 350°F. Place the bread in a shallow dish and add the milk; set aside.

Clean the anchovies, keeping the tail intact and opening them like a book (see instructions on page 104); rinse and pat dry. Dice 10 of the anchovies (discarding tails) and place them in a large bowl. Remove bread from milk, squeeze to release excess liquid, and break into small pieces; add to the bowl with chopped anchovies. Stir in the Parmigiano-Reggiano, eggs, parsley, marjoram, garlic, a generous pinch of salt, and a few grinds of black pepper, and mix thoroughly. The mixture should be thick enough to keep its shape, but not stiff or dry; if it feels too wet, add a tablespoon or two of breadcrumbs.

Line a large baking sheet with parchment paper and drizzle with olive oil.

Lay one butterflied anchovy flat on a clean work surface, skin side down, spoon 1 ½ to 2 teaspoons of filling on top of the fish, spreading to cover the entire fillet. Cover with another butterflied anchovy, skin side up, creating a little sandwich. Transfer to the prepared baking sheet and repeat with the rest of the anchovies and filling. Drizzle lightly with olive oil and sprinkle with 3 tablespoons of breadcrumbs.

Bake until golden brown, 10 to 12 minutes. Serve with lemon wedges.

Zuppa di Muscoli

Mussels Soup

3 pounds mussels

Extra-virgin olive oil

1 medium yellow onion, finely
    chopped

2 cloves garlic, minced,
    plus 1 whole clove, peeled

2 tablespoons finely chopped
    flat-leaf parsley

¾ cup dry white wine

1 14-ounce can crushed tomatoes

4-6 slices of toasted rustic
    Italian bread

Serves 4 to 6

This classic recipe is packed with flavor, yet quick and easy to prepare, especially if you buy farmed mussels, which are usually clean and debearded. Be sure to discard any mussels that are cracked when you buy them, and ones that don't open up after cooking.

♦ Clean the mussels: Scrub their shells with a brush, rinse thoroughly, and drain. If necessary, pull off any brown fibers between the two shells (also known as the beard) with a pair of tweezers or your fingers.

Place the mussels in a large, heavy-bottomed pot over high heat. Cover tightly and cook until mussels have opened, 5 to 6 minutes, shaking the pot once or twice in the meantime. Transfer the mussels to a large bowl, discarding any that haven't opened. Filter the cooking liquid with a fine mesh sieve and set aside; discard solids.

Rinse the pot and place over medium-high heat. Add 2 tablespoons olive oil; add the onion and cook until translucent, about 5 minutes. Add minced garlic and 1 tablespoon parsley and stir until fragrant, about 1 minute. Add ½ cup filtered cooking liquid, the white wine, and crushed tomatoes. Bring to a boil, then lower heat and simmer, uncovered, for 10 minutes, adding a splash of mussels' cooking liquid if too much liquid evaporates. Return mussels to the pot, cover, and cook just until heated through.

Cut the clove of garlic in half and rub the slices of bread with the cut side; place one slice in the bottom of each individual serving bowl. Arrange mussels over the bread and pour in a ladleful of broth. Garnish with the remaining parsley and serve immediately.

Branzino alla Ligure

Ligurian-style Sea Bass

Extra-virgin olive oil

1 ¾ pounds russet potatoes,
  peeled, halved, and thinly sliced

Salt

4 whole sea bass, each about
  1 ½ pounds, cleaned

4 small sprigs of rosemary

4 sprigs marjoram

4 cloves garlic, peeled

2 slices of lemon, halved

3 tablespoons Taggiasche
  or Niçoise olives

12 cherry tomatoes

2 tablespoons pine nuts

Serves 4

Cooking whole fish is easier than you may think and particularly reward-ing when baked on a bed of thinly sliced potatoes paired with pine nuts, Taggiasche olives, cherry tomatoes, and fresh herbs.

♦ Preheat the oven to 400°F. Line a large, rimmed baking sheet with parch-ment paper and drizzle with olive oil. Arrange the potato slices in an even layer in the baking sheet. Drizzle potatoes with a thin veil of olive oil and sprinkle generously with salt.

Rinse the fish under cold water and pat dry with paper towels. Season the cavity and outside of fish with salt. Stuff each fish's cavity with 1 sprig rosemary, 1 sprig of marjoram, 1 clove of garlic, and half of a lemon slice. Lay the fish on top of potatoes, leaving some space between each fish. Scatter olives, tomatoes, and pine nuts all around them. Drizzle lightly with olive oil and bake in preheated oven for about 20 minutes, or until the thickest part of the fish is firm and flakes away when poked with a sharp knife.

Stoccafisso

Stockfish

It seems ironic that stockfish, air-dried cod from northern Europe, would be so popular in Liguria. Why a coastal region, with direct access to the Mediterranean, would favor a dried fish from the other side of Europe seems baffling. Yet there are records of stockfish from Scandinavia finding its way to Genoa as early as the thirteenth century. As the city transformed into a powerful maritime empire, Genoa enjoyed a near monopoly over the Atlantic cod trade. The dried fish's long shelf life made it a favorite for long sea voyages. And so, stockfish found a permanent place at the Ligurian table.

Baccalà, which is salt-cured cod, also found its way to Genoa through the Portuguese, though it is less popular in the region than stockfish. To make the story a little more confusing, Venetians refer to stockfish as baccalà, so their famous dish of *baccalà mantecato* is actually made from stockfish.

In Genoa, head to the historic Bottega dello Stoccafisso, in the twisting alleyways of the city's center, where dried cod hangs from the walls and soaks in wide marble tubs. Both stockfish and baccalà need to be rehydrated in running water for several days before cooking, but in the specialty shops and fish markets of Italy you can often buy them presoaked. If you can only get your hands on the dried fish, place in a large bowl or pot and cover with cold water, then place in the refrigerator. Change water frequently, at least three times a day, and more often if possible, until fish is rehydrated and soft. For stockfish this will take four to five days, while salt cod will be ready in twenty-four to forty-eight hours.

My favorite advice about the fish comes from the writings of Umberto Curti, gastronome and culinary historian from Genoa: "Though stockfish was born in water, it must die in oil." So however you are preparing the dish, remember not to skimp on the extra-virgin olive oil.

Stoccafisso Accomodato

Stockfish and Potato Stew

With a shelf life of several years, dried stockfish was a favorite both on long sea voyages and in port cities like Genoa. This ancient Genovese recipe pairs dried cod with potatoes, pine nuts, and olives for a hearty, flavorful seafarer's stew. Try to get your hands on presoaked stockfish to cut down on days of prep time, otherwise see page 113 for soaking instructions.

4 medium Yukon gold potatoes,
    peeled and cut into large cubes
2 pounds presoaked stockfish
1 tablespoon white wine vinegar
3 tablespoons extra-virgin olive oil,
    plus more for serving
4 oil-packed anchovy fillets
1 large carrot, diced
1 large celery rib, diced
1 large white or yellow onion, diced
2 cloves garlic, minced
2 tablespoons flat-leaf parsley
2 tablespoons pine nuts
1 tablespoon salted capers, rinsed
20 Taggiasche or Niçoise olives pitted
⅓ cup dry white wine
5 ripe plum tomatoes, chopped

Serves 6

♦ Fill a large bowl with cold water and stir in a teaspoon of salt; add the potato pieces and set aside.

Bring a large pot of water to boil, add stockfish and vinegar, and cook for 5 to 10 minutes, or until the bones and skin come apart easily from the flesh. Drain fish and discard cooking water. When cool enough to handle, remove skin and pin bones, cut fish into large chunks, and set aside.

Heat olive oil in a large skillet or Dutch oven over medium-low heat, add anchovies and cook over low heat, stirring often, until they dissolve, 3 to 5 minutes. Add carrot, celery, and onion; cook over medium heat until onion is translucent and beginning to brown around the edges, 5 to 7 minutes.

Add fish pieces, garlic, and 1 tablespoon parsley. Cook over high heat for a couple minutes, then add pine nuts, capers, olives, and wine. Bring to a boil, add chopped tomatoes, cover and simmer over low heat for 1 hour, stirring occasionally and adding a splash of hot water as necessary to keep fish from sticking to the bottom of the pan.

Add potatoes and a pinch of salt. Cover and continue to cook until potatoes are soft and creamy, adding a splash of water if fish and potatoes are dry, about 45 minutes.

Add salt and pepper to taste, garnish with remaining tablespoon of parsley, drizzle with olive oil, and serve warm.

Cappon Magro

Ligurian Seafood Feast

At first glance, this extravagant dish seems contradictory to the understated elegance of Ligurian cuisine. Don't be fooled, *cappon magro* is about as Genovese as you can get. Remember, while rural Liguria might have been just scraping by, Genoa was a cosmopolitan, maritime power and center of trade from the thirteenth to the seventeenth centuries. Though born from humble beginnings (leftover boiled vegetables and fish were layered between vinegar-soaked hardtack to bulk up an otherwise meager meal), it was transformed by Genoa's upper class into an ornate, celebratory dish. Piled high into a complex dome, adorned with shrimp, olives, hard-boiled eggs, lobster, and occasionally raw oysters, this pageant on a plate echoes the Baroque palaces of Genoa's aristocratic families.

Today *cappon magro* still makes its way to the Ligurian table on Christmas Eve, and it's certain to be a showstopper on your table too, at any time of the year. There are many ways to assemble the dish: Some use a loaf tin or bowl as a mold, some construct a pyramid shape from the bottom up, others use a ring mold to assemble smaller, individual *cappon magro* on each serving plate. I personally love the vintage look of a dome so I suggest using an 8-inch bowl as the mold.

Note: See page 182 for more information about *Gallette del Marinaio*.

For the green sauce:

2 slices of stale or lightly toasted white sandwich bread, crusts removed

3 tablespoons white wine vinegar

4 oil-packed anchovy fillets

2 cups packed flat-leaf parsley leaves

⅓ cup (about 1 ½ ounces) pine nuts

½ clove of garlic

2 tablespoons salted capers, rinsed

2 hard-boiled egg yolks

¾ cup extra-virgin olive oil

Salt to taste

Continued...

♦ Prepare the green sauce: Place the bread in a wide, shallow bowl, sprinkle with 2 tablespoons vinegar and 1 tablespoon water; soak for 5 minutes. Squeeze bread with your hands to remove excess liquid, then transfer to a blender or food processor. Add anchovy fillets, parsley leaves, pine nuts, garlic, capers, hard-boiled egg yolks, and 1 tablespoon vinegar; blend until smooth. While machine is running, add the oil through the feeder tube in a slow, steady stream until thoroughly combined. Transfer the sauce to a bowl, cover and refrigerate until ready to use. (You may make the sauce 1 day in advance.)

♦ Prepare the dome: Rinse the whole fish, inside and out, and place in a large, wide skillet or an oval-shaped Dutch oven. Cover with enough cold water to completely submerge the fish, add 1 tablespoon salt and bring to a simmer over medium-high heat, but don't let it come to a rolling boil. Adjust heat to maintain a slow simmer until the flesh of the fish is opaque and flakes easily with a knife when poked, about 20 minutes (start testing for doneness

Continued...

after 15 minutes). Remove fish from liquid; set aside until cool enough to handle. Carefully clean the fish, removing all skin and pin bones; collect the flesh in a bowl, cover, and refrigerate until ready to use.

Place the whole beet in a steamer basket set over 1 inch of boiling water, cover, and steam until beet is soft when pierced with a fork, 30 to 45 minutes depending on size. Remove from steamer. When cool enough to handle peel, and cut into ⅛-inch-thick rounds.

Meanwhile, place the peeled, whole potatoes in a large pot of generously salted water and bring to boil over medium-high heat. Cook until soft but not falling apart; remove potatoes with a slotted spoon and set aside. Bring water back to a boil. Prepare an ice bath in a large bowl. Boil the zucchini until fork tender, then transfer immediately to ice bath with a slotted spoon; when cool, drain and set aside in a small bowl. Repeat this process with the green beans and carrots, boiling and cooling each vegetable separately. Set each vegetable aside in separate bowls. Shell and cut the shrimp into bite-sized chunks; set aside. Slice the potatoes into ¼-inch-thick rounds; set aside.

Rub the *gallette del marinaio* all over with the garlic and place in a wide, shallow bowl. Stir together the vinegar and water and sprinkle the mixture over the biscuits; set aside.

Line an 8-inch bowl (or mold of choice) with plastic wrap, leaving some overhang on all sides. Place half the potato slices in the bottom of the bowl in a single layer, only filling about 1 ½ inches of the bottom; press lightly with your hands. Spread a thin layer of sauce over the potatoes and cover with a layer of zucchini; press lightly to compact the vegetables then spread with another thin layer of sauce. Continue layering the vegetables, alternating with cooked fish and shrimp, spreading a thin layer of sauce between each one. Reserve some sliced zucchini and carrots for the final garnish. You may layer the ingredients in any order you choose; just keep in mind to alternate colors in order for the best visual impact. Finish with a layer of vinegar-soaked *gallette del marinaio*. Press lightly to flatten; cover with plastic wrap and refrigerate, flat side up, for at least 1 hour or overnight.

♦ To finish: Place the mussels in a large, heavy bottomed pot over high heat. Cover tightly and cook until mussels have opened, 5 to 6 minutes, shaking the pot once or twice in the meantime. Transfer the mussels to a large bowl and discard any that haven't opened.

♦ To unmold the dome: Place a wide, beautiful serving platter on top of the bowl. Hold onto the platter and invert the bowl. Lift the bowl and remove the plastic wrap from the dome. Decorate with zucchini and carrot rounds. Place the lobster or langoustines on top of the dome and arrange shrimp around them. Arrange hard-boiled eggs, olives, and mussels around the base of the dome. Serve at room temperature with green sauce on the side.

For the dome:

1 whole, large sea bass or sea bream, about 2 ¼ pounds, cleaned

Salt

1 beet, tops trimmed, scrubbed

¾ pound baking potatoes, peeled (about 2 medium potatoes)

¾ pound zucchini, sliced into ¼-inch coins (about 2 medium zucchini)

½ pound green beans (about 2 ½ cups), trimmed and cut into 1-inch pieces

1 pound carrots, peeled and sliced into coins ⅛-inch thick (about 5 medium carrots)

5 *gallette del marinaio* (see note)

½ clove garlic

3 tablespoons white wine vinegar

3 tablespoons water

½ pound large/jumbo shrimp, boiled and shelled

To finish:

12 mussels, scrubbed and debearded

1 lobster, about 1 pound or langostino, boiled or steamed and chilled

6 jumbo red shrimp or prawns, boiled or steamed and chilled

4 hard boiled eggs, peeled and quartered

10 large green or black olives, pitted

Serves 6

Carne

·

Meat

It's no coincidence that this is the shortest chapter in this book. Historically, meat was scarce in Liguria and, except for the upper-class families in wealthy Genoa, never accounted for a significant part of the local diet. Instead, meat was used almost as a seasoning: Small amounts added flavor and depth to ravioli, *ripieni*, and baked goods. Unlike elsewhere in Italy, in Liguria, meat is never alone; it's always accompanied by vegetables, herbs, sauces, and side dishes — only one of the many players in the symphony that is a typical local meal.

Antica Polleria Anna e Sergio, Genoa

Coniglio alla Ligure

Ligurian-style Rabbit

You will find this iconic dish on the menu of every self-respecting, family-style, countryside trattoria in Liguria. Easy to raise, quick to reproduce, and requiring limited space to house, rabbit rapidly became the livestock of choice in the harsh Ligurian hills. When stewed slowly with white wine and the flavors of local ingredients like olives and pine nuts, the naturally lean meat becomes juicy and irresistible. If sold whole, ask your butcher to cut the rabbit into pieces for you and remove the head. If you like, request the kidneys and liver, which add an extra level of flavor. This is one of my kids' favorites, as the subtly flavored, tender, white meat is similar to chicken. Not a fan of rabbit? You may substitute three and a half pounds of chicken thighs and drumsticks, just reduce the cooking time to forty minutes.

♦   Heat olive oil in a skillet over medium-high heat. Set aside rabbit kidneys and liver, if using. Season rabbit pieces all over with salt and cook, turning occasionally, until they are golden brown all over, about 10 to 15 minutes. Add garlic cloves and cook, stirring frequently, until fragrant, about 3 minutes. Tie the rosemary with kitchen twine so it doesn't lose its needles. Add rosemary, bay leaf, olives, and pine nuts to the skillet; pour in wine and bring to a boil, allowing the alcohol to evaporate slightly, about 2 minutes. Pour in chicken broth. Bring to a boil; lower to a gentle simmer and cook, stirring occasionally until the meat is very tender and pulling away from the bones, about 1 hour to 1 hour and 10 minutes. If all the liquid evaporates while cooking, you may add a splash of water as needed to avoid sticking. Meanwhile, season the liver and kidneys with salt. Heat 1 tablespoon of olive oil in a separate small skillet, add giblets, and cook, turning once until nicely browned, about 1 minute per side. Add giblets to rabbit mixture for the last 10 minutes of cooking. When ready to serve, remove bay leaf and rosemary. Serve rabbit warm in the skillet, with pan juices, pine nuts, and olives.

5 tablespoons extra-virgin olive oil

1 whole rabbit (about 3 ½ pounds) cut into pieces, with giblets (optional)

3 cloves garlic, peeled

1 sprig rosemary

1 bay leaf

2 tablespoons pine nuts

½ cup dry white wine

½ cup homemade vegetable or chicken broth

⅓ cup Taggiasche or Niçoise olives, pitted or not

Serves 2 to 4

Tócco

Pot Roast and Pasta Sauce

Tócco means "chunk" or "piece" in local dialect, and when Ligurians actually got their hands on a large piece of meat, they really put it to work. In this classic recipe, a chuck roast is slow-cooked in aromatics and wine until tender. The resulting sauce is used to dress ravioli or other pasta dishes, and then the roast is sliced thin and served as a second course, or repurposed for making meatballs, ravioli, or even stuffed vegetables. Try this with the *Ravioli di Carne con Tócco* recipe on page 70.

♦ Place the dried mushrooms in a small bowl and cover with hot water. Set aside to rehydrate for 30 minutes. Strain and finely chop the mushrooms; reserve ½ cup soaking liquid.

⅓ oz dried porcini mushrooms

4 tablespoons extra virgin olive oil

1 ½ pounds chuck roast

1 large stalk of celery, finely minced

1 medium onion, finely minced

2 large carrots, finely minced
  or grated

¾ cup dry white wine

Salt

2 tablespoons tomato paste

1 bay leaf

1 sprig of rosemary, tied with
  kitchen twine

5 sage leaves

Serves 6

Heat the olive oil in a stockpot or earthenware cooking pot over medium heat. Add the meat and cook, turning occasionally, until well browned all over, 10 to 15 minutes. Season meat all over with ¼ teaspoon salt, lower heat, and add minced vegetables. Sauté, stirring often, until vegetables are soft, about 10 minutes. Add mushrooms, the mushroom soaking liquid, wine, ½ teaspoon salt, and tomato paste; bring to a boil. Add broth, bay leaf, rosemary, sage, and bring to a boil over medium heat. Lower heat to maintain a slow simmer, cover tightly, and cook for at least 3 hours, turning the meat every 30 minutes or so. If the liquid evaporates and the meat begins to stick, add a splash of water occasionally to retain some sauce. The meat should be tender enough to break apart easily with a fork. Remove roast from the pot and slice thinly to serve, or set aside for another use (such as the filling for the ravioli on page 70 or *Tomaxèlle* on page 133). Discard bay leaf and rosemary. Taste sauce and add more salt if necessary. If it is too watery, reduce it over medium-high heat until desired consistency is reached. Use sauce to dress pasta like *Picagge Verdi* on page 58 or *Ravioli di Carne con Tócco* on page 70.

Fritto Misto alla Ligure

Mixed Fried Things

For the stecchi (skewers):

3 slices stale or lightly toasted white
  sandwich bread, crusts removed

⅔ cup milk

Extra-virgin olive oil

2 pounds boneless veal or pork
  loin, cut into 1-inch chunks

Salt

3 large eggs

1 egg yolk from a large egg

1 ounce finely grated Parmigiano-
  Reggiano (about ¼ cup, packed)

⅔ cup plain breadcrumbs

Vegetable or grapeseed oil, for frying

Special equipment:

8 6-inch wooden skewers

For the cotolette (cutlets):

4 very thin slices of beef (top round)

1 large egg, lightly beaten

⅓ cup plain breadcrumbs

Extra-virgin olive oil, for frying

To finish:

Fritti di Verdura (see page 146)

Latte Fritto (see page 205)

Lemon wedges, for serving

Serves 4 to 6

My husband, Emilio, has quite a convincing way of describing fried foods as "light" when they're anything but. He can't help it; it is in his blood. Ligurians are expert fryers, and the ultimate compliment for a local chef is that their fried foods are *leggeri*. This is clearly not in reference to the calorie count but to the mouthfeel. The crust of fried foods should be crunchy and shatter beneath your teeth, but the batter must be light as a cloud, not greasy. Nowhere does Liguria's frying talent shine like in their famous *fritto misto*. This extravagant feast combines tempura-like, crisp vegetables with paper-thin cutlets, mysterious meat skewers, and sweet, fried custard. Home cooks rarely go to the trouble of preparing this elaborate platter, but it's a standard in trattorias and restaurants around the region.

Dinner at our favorite local spot, Trattoria Pagliettini, is a marathon. We start with *Antipasto Misto* (see page 37) and house vermentino before moving on to a taste of three *primi* (*Trenette al Pesto*, page 69, *Pansoti con Salsa di Noci*, page 81, and *Ravioli di Magro*, page 73). My pants are tight and my head is spinning by the time the waiter asks what we would like for *secondo*. I can't possibly eat another bite, but I know I'm in for another treat when Emilio turns to me and inquires innocently, "Shall we split a *fritto misto*? It's very light."

♦   For the stecchi: Place the bread slices in a wide, shallow dish and add the milk; set aside to soak. Heat 2 tablespoons of olive oil in a skillet or frying pan over medium-high heat. When hot, add the veal cubes and cook, stirring occasionally, until meat is golden brown on all sides, 7 to 9 minutes. Salt to taste and set meat aside to cool. When cool enough to handle, transfer about ⅓ of the veal to a food processor; set aside. Thread remaining veal cubes onto 8 wooden skewers, leaving at least 1 inch of skewer free on both ends. Remove bread from milk; squeeze to wring out all excess liquid, and add to the food processor. Add 1 egg, the egg yolk, Parmigiano, and ½ teaspoon salt to the food processor and pulse until well combined. Pour the mixture into a wide, shallow bowl or dish and turn the skewered veal in the mixture. Use damp hands to press the blended mixture around the meat until all the cubes are completely covered by the mixture.

Continued...

Crack remaining 2 eggs into a wide, shallow dish, add a dash of salt, and beat lightly with a fork; pour breadcrumbs onto a separate plate. Carefully tip each skewer first into the beaten egg, then roll in the breadcrumbs, pressing to adhere.

Heat 1 inch of oil in a wide, deep skillet, until a pinch of breadcrumbs sizzles immediately upon contact with the hot oil. Fry the skewers, a few at a time, turning occasionally, until golden brown and crisp, 3 to 4 minutes. Drain on a paper towel-lined plate. Serve immediately.

♦ For the *cotolette*: Crack the egg into a shallow dish, add a dash of salt, and beat lightly with a fork; pour breadcrumbs onto a separate plate. Place a slice of meat in the egg mixture, turning to coat and covering it completely; shake to drip off excess. Coat the meat completely in the breadcrumbs, pressing to adhere. Repeat with remaining meat.

Pour enough oil in a frying pan to come up ¼ inch up the sides of the pan. Heat on medium-high until oil is shiny and a breadcrumb sizzles when it touches the hot oil. Working in batches as necessary to avoid crowding the pan, add a couple of cutlets to the pan and fry, flipping once, when golden brown and crisp, about 3 minutes per side. Season with salt and transfer to a plate and keep warm while you fry remaining cutlets.

♦ Assemble platter: Arrange fried vegetables, *Latte fritto*, *stecchi*, and *cotolette* on a large platter. Garnish with lemon wedges and serve hot.

Tomaxèlle

Stuffed Veal Rolls

1 ounce dried porcini mushrooms
  (about 1 cup)

2 slices stale or lightly toasted white
  sandwich bread, crusts removed

½ cup milk

3 ½ ounces ground veal or beef
  (or ½ cup diced, leftover
  cooked meat)

1 ½ ounces finely grated Parmigiano-
  Reggiano (about
  ½ cup, packed)

1 clove garlic, minced

2 tablespoons pine nuts, chopped

1 teaspoon finely chopped marjoram

2 teaspoons finely chopped flat-leaf
  parsley

1 pinch of nutmeg

2 large eggs, lightly beaten

12 paper-thin slices of veal loin (about
  24 ounces total)

3 tablespoons unsalted butter

½ cup dry white wine

½ cup homemade beef broth
  (see note on page 21)

1 tablespoon tomato paste

Salt and pepper

Serves 4

My mother-in-law, Fernanda, first made these for me when we were on lock-down in Moneglia together in 2020; this is her mother's recipe. This ancient dish is exemplary of Ligurian cuisine; a relatively small amount of meat is transformed into a hearty, satisfying meal. Originally designed to recycle leftover meat and vegetable scraps, a paper-thin slice of veal is covered with a savory mix of breadcrumbs, fresh herbs, pine nuts, and Parmigiano, then rolled into a small bundle and simmered in a flavorful sauce. If you have left-over meat (for instance, from *Tócco*, page 126), finely dice it and substitute a half cup of it for the ground veal.

♦   Place dried mushrooms in a small bowl, cover with hot water, and set aside to soak for 15 minutes. Place bread slices in a wide, shallow dish and add milk. Turn to coat and let soak for 10 minutes. Drain mushrooms and squeeze to release excess water. Chop the mushrooms and place them in a large bowl. Remove bread from milk, squeeze to wring out excess liquid, tear into small pieces, and add to the bowl. Add ground veal, Parmigiano-Reggiano, garlic, pine nuts, marjoram, parsley, nutmeg, and eggs. Season with salt and pepper and mix until well combined.

Lay the veal slices out on a clean work surface and spread about a table-spoon of filling in the center of one slice. Roll the slice into a little burrito shape, tucking in the sides and securing with kitchen twine or a toothpick. Repeat with remaining veal slices and filling.

Melt the butter in a large saucepan over medium heat. Add the veal rolls and cook, turning occasionally until golden on all sides, about 6 minutes. Deglaze with the wine and scrape up any brown bits stuck to the pan. Add broth and tomato paste. Bring to a boil, then lower heat so liquid is at a gentle simmer, stirring occasionally and adding a tablespoon of water as necessary, until sauce has thickened and rolls are cooked through, about 20 minutes. Taste for salt and adjust seasonings as desired. Serve warm.

Costolette d'Agnello Fritte

Fried Lamb Cutlets

8 single-rib lamb chops

Salt and freshly ground black pepper

1 cup fine plain breadcrumbs

2 large eggs

1 ¼ ounces finely grated Parmigiano-
Reggiano (about
⅓ cup, packed)

Vegetable oil, for frying

Lemon wedges, for serving

Serves 4

This is one of the many recipes I coaxed out of Zia Marghe, and it's one of her favorites to prepare for Easter. While this dish isn't unique to Liguria, it's a classic for our family and for many others in the region. Easter is of huge cultural, not to mention religious, importance in Italy, and is celebrated with elaborate meals and specific dishes like this one and the *Torta Pasqualina* on page 157. Seek out high-quality, grass-fed lamb from your butcher for this recipe.

♦ Lay the chops on a cutting board and pound with a meat mallet until they are as thin as possible, without breaking or tearing. Salt and pepper both sides of each lamb chop. Pour breadcrumbs into a shallow dish. Break eggs into a separate shallow dish and beat lightly with a fork; add Parmigiano and stir to combine. Turn a lamb chop in the egg mixture, covering it completely; shake to drip off excess. Coat the chop completely in the breadcrumbs, pressing to adhere. Repeat with remaining meat.

Pour enough oil in a frying pan to come up ¼ inch up the sides of the pan. Heat on medium-high until oil is shiny and a crumb of bread sizzles when it touches the hot oil. Working in batches, place a few chops in the pan and fry, flipping once, until golden brown and crisp, about 3 minutes per side. Sprinkle with salt and transfer to a platter and keep warm while you continue frying remaining chops. Add lemon wedges to the platter and serve right away.

Pollo in Fricassea

Chicken Fricassee

3 tablespoons extra-virgin olive oil

1 whole chicken (3 ½ to 4 pounds),
   cut into pieces

Salt

Freshly ground black pepper

2 tablespoons unsalted butter

1 small yellow onion, finely diced

1 celery stalk, finely diced

1 medium carrot, finely diced

1 ½ tablespoons all-purpose flour

¾ cup dry white wine

2 ½ cups chicken broth

5 fresh sage leaves

2 large egg yolks, room temperature

2 tablespoons fresh lemon juice

1 teaspoon diced flat-leaf parsley

1 teaspoon diced fresh marjoram

Serves 4

Versions of *fricassea* (also known as fricassee or fricassée) can be found all over. In Italy, the sauce is thickened with an egg and lemon emulsion, added after the chicken has cooked through. Feel free to substitute the chicken with rabbit or veal, which are both popular variations in Liguria.

♦ Heat 2 tablespoons of olive oil in a skillet over medium-high heat. Season chicken pieces all over with salt and pepper and cook, turning occasionally, until they are golden brown all over, about 10 to 15 minutes. Remove from pan and set aside. Add butter and 1 tablespoon olive oil to the pan (do not clean the pan) and melt over medium heat. Add onion, celery, and carrot and continue to cook until onion is translucent, about 7 minutes. Add flour and cook, stirring constantly, for 2 minutes. Slowly add wine and broth, then stir constantly, scraping up bits from the bottom of the pan with a spatula, until combined. Add salt to taste. Add sage and chicken pieces, along with any juices that have collected on the plate. Bring to a boil and then lower heat to maintain a steady simmer until the juices run clear when chicken is pierced near the bone, or internal temperature reaches 165°F, about 20 minutes.

Whisk together egg yolks and lemon juice in a small bowl until smooth. Very slowly pour in 1 cup of hot cooking liquid, whisking constantly until smooth. Remove chicken from heat and slowly add egg mixture to pot, stirring constantly. Turn the chicken pieces in the sauce and add parsley and marjoram; serve hot.

Verdure

◆

Vegetables

The warm climate and fertile soil in Liguria create the perfect conditions for vegetable gardens. Take a quick drive outside any touristy beach town on a switchbacked road toward the hills, and you'll be surprised how many terraced backyard gardens you spot before you leave the city limits. It's no surprise that this cuisine relies heavily on plant-forward dishes, using meat as a flavoring rather than as the main attraction.

Even I, with my famously non-green thumb, was able to grow a surprisingly productive garden while marooned in Moneglia for the fateful spring of 2020 during our first COVID-19 lockdown. In Texas, gardening is a war against the elements; a constant struggle against searing heat, parching droughts, blights, insects, and the catastrophic, unexpected hard freeze. In Liguria, it is a dance. You plant something, and it just grows. I couldn't believe my eyes: My little organic plot was soon overflowing with colossal cabbages, sprawling artichoke plants, leafy chard, bright red radishes, and carrots. As spring stretched into summer I was rewarded with plump *cuore di bue* tomatoes, shiny bell peppers, flawless little strawberries, white and purple striped eggplants, fresh lettuces, and fragrant basil.

Amazingly, as prolific as our garden proved to be, nothing ever went to waste. The *nonne* deftly transformed countless baskets of ripe tomatoes into salads, sauces, or stuffed and baked them. Zucchini went into risotto, or it was stuffed, sliced, fried, or pickled. The eggplant was grilled, sautéed, diced, fried, added to pasta sauces or meat dishes. The Ligurian ability of inserting vegetables into every dish is unsurpassed.

This chapter explores some of Liguria's most iconic vegetarian sides and mains. When vegetables take center stage it's important to focus on their quality, so be sure to procure the freshest, preferably organic, produce as possible.

Ripieni di Verdura

Stuffed Vegetables

Ripieni di verdura are yet another prime example of the endless Ligurian flair for stuffed foods. Depending on the area, meat or prosciutto is sometimes added to the filling but is by no means necessary. In this popular version, dried porcini mushrooms provide the umami, but you could easily substitute them with other dried mushrooms if necessary. Serve as an unexpected appetizer or as a colorful, vegetarian main course.

♦ Preheat oven to 375°F. Line 2 baking sheets with parchment paper and drizzle lightly with olive oil; set aside.

Place dried mushrooms in a small bowl and cover with warm water; set aside to soak until softened, about 15 minutes. Place bread slices in a wide, shallow dish and pour milk over. Set aside to soak.

Bring a large pot of generously salted water to boil over high heat. Meanwhile, cut the zucchini in half lengthwise (if using large zucchini, also cut them in half crosswise, to obtain 12 pieces). Boil zucchini until just tender but still al dente, 6 to 7 minutes. Transfer zucchini to a colander to cool slightly and return water to a boil. Cut onions in half crosswise and toss them into the pot. Boil until just tender, 7 to 8 minutes. Transfer onions to the colander with a slotted spoon. Clean peppers and cut lengthwise into quarters. Add them to the pot and boil until just tender, about 7 minutes.

Roughly dice 4 of the boiled zucchini pieces; set aside in a medium bowl. Use a small spoon to carefully scoop the flesh out of the remaining zucchini pieces to create little boats. Scoop the flesh into the bowl with the chopped zucchini. Transfer zucchini boats to the prepared baking sheet. Carefully hollow out the onion halves, leaving the outer two or three petals intact, to create a hollow onion half to be filled. Transfer the 4 hollow onion halves to the baking sheet. Chop the onion cores and transfer to the bowl with the zucchini flesh and pieces. Place the bell pepper quarters, skin side down, on the baking sheet. Remove mushrooms from soaking liquid, rinse and squeeze dry. Chop mushrooms and add to the bowl with the zucchini and chopped onion.

Heat 2 tablespoons of oil in a medium frying pan over medium-high heat, add garlic and zucchini mixture. Cook, stirring occasionally, until liquid has evaporated, 5 to 8 minutes. Remove from heat and let mixture cool slightly. Transfer to a food processor. Remove bread slices from milk, squeeze to wring out excess liquid and add to the food processor. Add eggs, marjoram, and ½ teaspoon salt. Pulse until well combined and almost smooth. Stir in Parmigiano-Reggiano. Spoon the filling into the vegetables on the baking sheet using a small spoon or pastry bag. Sprinkle with bread crumbs and bake until golden, about 30 minutes. Serve warm.

¼ cup dried porcini mushrooms
  (or other dried mushrooms)
4 slices stale or lightly toasted white
  sandwich bread, crusts removed
⅔ cup whole milk
6 small (or 3 large) zucchini
2 yellow onions, peeled
1 small yellow or red bell pepper
2 tablespoons extra-virgin olive oil
1 clove garlic, minced
2 large eggs
1 teaspoon marjoram
3 ½ ounces freshly grated
  Parmigiano-Reggiano (about
  1 cup, packed)
2 tablespoons plain breadcrumbs

Serves 4 to 6

Fritti di Verdura

Fried Vegetables

2 cups (9 ounces) all-purpose flour

½ teaspoon salt, plus more to taste

1 ¼ cup sparkling water

1 large egg

4 ice cubes

Vegetable or grapeseed oil,
   for frying

2 medium zucchinis, sliced very thinly
   lengthwise

1 medium eggplant, halved lengthwise
   and sliced thinly
   into half-moons

2 medium carrots, sliced very
   thinly lengthwise

1 small onion, halved and sliced

Serves 4 to 6

Crisp, light, airy fried veggies are a common sight in Liguria, and pairs the local love of frying with the abundant produce. Feel free to substitute the vegetables for whatever produce at peak: thinly sliced beets, broccoli, and cauliflower are delicious wintertime alternatives.

◆   Stir together flour and salt in a wide bowl. Slowly stir in sparkling water, a little at a time, stirring constantly with a whisk; the mixture should have the consistency of thin pancake batter. Whisk vigorously until very smooth; there should be no lumps in sight. Add the egg and stir until well combined. Add the ice cubes and transfer the batter to the refrigerator until ready to fry, up to 1 hour.

Pour about 2 inches of oil into a deep skillet or wok; heat over high heat until a drop of batter sizzles when it touches the oil. Working with a few pieces at a time, dip sliced vegetables in batter, then transfer directly to hot oil. Important: be careful not to drop any of the ice cubes into the hot oil. Cook until crisp and golden, 2 to 3 minutes. Use a spider or slotted spoon to remove fried vegetables from hot oil; transfer to paper towels to drain. Sprinkle with salt and repeat with remaining vegetables. Serve hot.

Verdure

Polpettone di Fagiolini e Patate

Potato and Green Bean Tart

18 ounces green beans
  (about 5 cups), trimmed and
  chopped into 1-inch pieces

1 ⅓ pounds (about 2 large) Russet
  or Yukon Gold potatoes, scrubbed

¼ cup extra-virgin olive oil, divided,
  plus more for pan

1 large or 2 small cloves of garlic,
  minced

1 tablespoon very finely chopped
  flat-leaf parsley

1 ½ teaspoons very finely chopped
  marjoram

⅛ teaspoon nutmeg

Salt and pepper to taste

3 ½ ounces finely grated Parmigiano-
  Reggiano (about
  1 cup, packed)

1 large egg, lightly beaten

1 large egg yolk

½ cup plain breadcrumbs

Serves 4 to 6

Leave it to Ligurians to take *polpettone* (which means "meatloaf" in the rest of Italy) and turn it into a vegetarian tart. When seasoned with fresh herbs and plenty of Parmigiano, this mashed-up mix of potatoes and green beans is transformed into a delightful plant-based side or main.

♦ Preheat oven to 350°F. Bring a medium pot of water to boil over medium-high heat. When boiling, salt generously and add green beans. Cook until tender but still bright green and slightly al dente, 7 to 9 minutes; drain and rinse under cold water. When cool enough to handle, dice green beans into small pieces; set aside.

Meanwhile, place potatoes in a separate pot and cover with cold water. Add 3 tablespoons salt and bring to a boil over high heat. Lower heat and simmer until potatoes are tender all the way through when poked with a sharp knife, between 10 and 20 minutes, depending on the size of your potatoes. Remove potatoes from water with a slotted spoon when they are ready and set aside until just cool enough to handle but still hot. Peel potatoes, break into chunks, and feed through a potato ricer into a large bowl. Alternatively, mash with a fork or potato masher.

Heat 1 tablespoon of olive oil in a medium skillet over medium-high heat. Add drained green beans and garlic and cook until fragrant, about 3 minutes. Transfer green bean mixture to the bowl with the mashed potatoes. Add parsley, marjoram, nutmeg, ½ teaspoon salt, and ¼ teaspoon pepper; set aside to cool. When mixture has cooled down a bit, add Parmigiano-Reggiano, then taste, adding more salt and pepper if desired. Stir in egg, yolk, and 3 tablespoons olive oil; mix well to combine.

Grease the bottom and sides of a 10-inch round tart pan or glass baking dish with olive oil and sprinkle with ¼ cup breadcrumbs, shaking to distribute them evenly around the bottom and sides of pan. Scoop potato mixture into the pan and spread evenly with a spatula. Etch a crosshatch pattern on the surface of the tart with the tines of a fork. Sprinkle with remaining breadcrumbs, drizzle with a little more olive oil, and bake until golden, about 25 minutes. Serve warm or at room temperature.

Spinaci alla Genovese

Genovese-style Spinach with Pine Nuts and Raisins

⅓ cup raisins

2 pounds fresh spinach, washed

2 tablespoons extra-virgin olive oil

3 oil-packed anchovy fillets

1 clove garlic, peeled

⅓ cup pine nuts

1 teaspoon chopped flat-leaf parsley,
  optional

Serves 4

This simple recipe perfectly demonstrates how a few clever flavor pairings can brighten up any vegetable recipe. The sweetness of the raisins, the buttery crunch of the pine nuts, and the umami of the anchovies transform a plain dish of steamed spinach into a delightful side dish.

♦ Place the raisins in a small bowl and cover with hot water. Let sit at room temperature for at least 30 minutes or until soft. Before using, drain raisins and squeeze out excess liquid with your hands.

Place a steamer basket in a large pot filled with ½ inch of boiling water. Add the spinach, cover, and steam for 5 minutes, or until wilted. Remove from pot and let cool in a colander. When cool enough to handle, squeeze the spinach with your hands to remove excess liquid. Transfer to a cutting board and chop a few times to break up the leaves (but do not chop finely).

Heat the olive oil in a large skillet over medium-high heat. Add the anchovy filets and cook until they mostly dissolve, about 1 minute. Add the whole clove of garlic, spinach, raisins, pine nuts, and a pinch of salt; stir to combine. Sauté over high heat until fragrant, and all liquid has evaporated, for 5 to 7 minutes. Garnish with parsley, if desired, and serve warm.

Fiori di Zucca Ripieni

Stuffed Squash Blossoms

Growing up in Texas, my mother's garden brimmed over with zucchini and summer squashes, but I only discovered squash blossoms after moving to Italy. Although my family transformed the overly abundant vegetables into endless dishes (zucchini bread, anyone?), the blossoms remained untouched. Summers in Italy, on the other hand, overflow with *fiori di zucca*. You'll find them in frittatas, risottos, salads, pastas, and pizzas, raw, fried, or oven-roasted. I love to fry them in the same airy batter I use for *Salvia Fritta* (page 30) or *Fritti di Verdura* (page 146). In Liguria, of course, you'll often find them stuffed with a fresh, herb-packed filling. However they're prepared, these delicate blossoms are, in my mind, one of Italy's most elegant foods.

12 zucchini or squash blossoms

1 ½ cups peeled and chopped Russet or
    Yukon Gold potatoes potatoes

Salt

1 cup finely chopped zucchini

¾ cup fresh green beans, chopped into
    ½-inch pieces

1 large egg

1 ounce finely grated Parmigiano-
    Reggiano (about ¼ cup, packed)

1 teaspoon of marjoram leaves,
    finely chopped

1 tablespoon of fresh flat-leaf parsley,
    finely chopped

½ clove of garlic, grated or minced

freshly ground pepper

2 tablespoons extra-virgin olive oil

2 tablespoons plain breadcrumbs

Serves 4

♦ Wash the zucchini flowers very gently under cold running water, being careful not to break or bruise them. Remove the stamen from inside of each flower and place the blossoms on a clean kitchen towel to dry.

Place the potatoes in a medium saucepan and cover with cold water; add a teaspoon of salt and bring to a boil over medium-high heat. Boil for 2 to 3 minutes, then add chopped zucchini and green beans. Continue to cook over medium heat until vegetables are fork-tender, 7 to 10 minutes. Drain vegetables and transfer to a large bowl. Smash with a fork or potato masher until you form a dense paste. Add egg, Parmigiano-Reggiano, marjoram, parsley, garlic, ¼ teaspoon salt, and pepper to taste; stir to combine.

Preheat oven to 350°F. The easiest way to fill the flowers is to use a pastry bag with a wide, round tip, but if you don't have one you may use two small spoons to scoop the mixture inside the flowers. Open the flower petals of each blossom and very carefully fill them with the potato mixture, making sure not to fill the flowers more than ¾ of the way full. Gently close the petals, twisting them slightly to hold the filling in place. Arrange the stuffed blossoms on a parchment-lined baking sheet. Carefully brush the surface of the flowers evenly with olive oil and dust with breadcrumbs and a pinch of salt.

Bake for 15 to 20 minutes, or until golden and puffy. Serve hot.

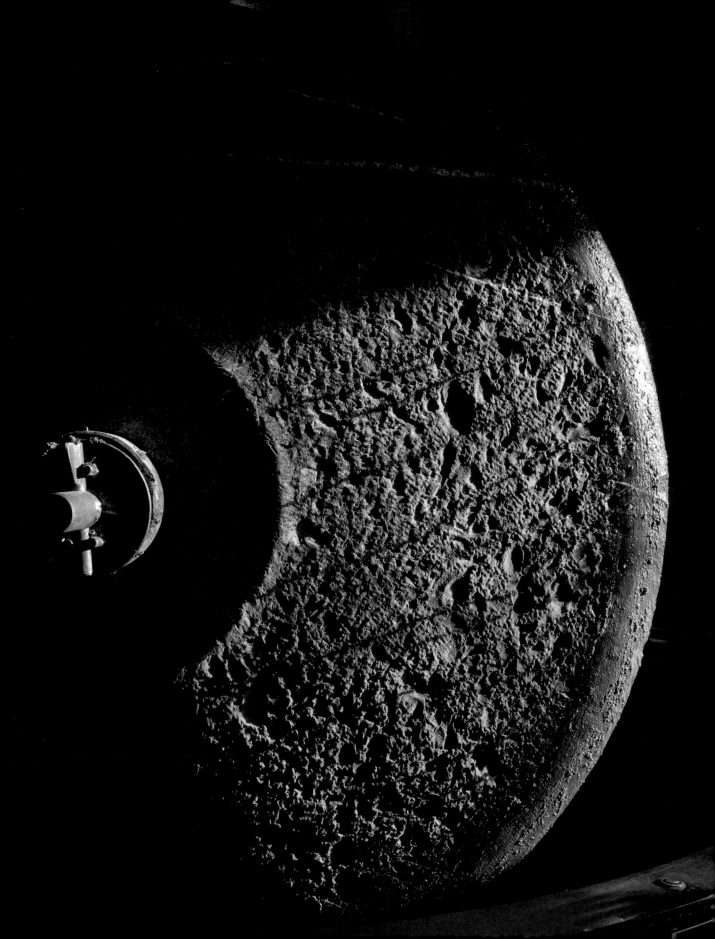

Olio Extravergine d'Oliva

Extra-virgin Olive Oil

"People think we just turn it on for show when tourists show up," Giada frowns, indicating the massive stone olive mill in the center of the room, its bulky granite millstones patiently grinding down a half-ton of olives in its hewn rock tub, with the impossible, hulking grace of an elephant. "But this is really how we make our oil, just like my grandfather did."

We are chatting in the Dinoabbo headquarters in Lucinasco, an ancient village in the hills surrounding Imperia, which are particularly favorable to olive production because of geographical position, climate, and altitude. Olive groves dominate the landscape so much here that when the wind blows and the leaves reveal their silvery underbellies, entire hill-sides shimmer. We are in the midst of harvest season, and the grassy smell of freshly crushed olives in the workshop is almost intoxicating. The old mill grinds tirelessly, nearly every day between October and January. Giada explains what makes Ligurian extra virgin olive oil so special. Small in size with a sweet, delicate flavor, the local *Taggiasca* olives are responsible for Imperia's aromatic and fruity oil, so coveted around the world. The port city began exporting the product in the mid-1800s, and Imperia is still considered the world's extra virgin olive oil capital.

The history of Liguria is inextricably interwoven with olive oil; it has been the lifeblood of the region for centuries. My mother-in-law remembers how, during the most destitute times of World War II, her father would cart their homegrown olive oil to Piemonte and trade it for flour, poultry, and other rare commodities. We still collect olives from those same trees in

Moneglia and make our own oil every autumn. All the cousins come together for a weekend of late nights eating and drinking, and early mornings of amateur manual labor. It's not a large or particularly efficient operation, nothing like Dinoabbo's. We only produce enough oil for each family to take home a few bottles, but we enjoy the experience just as much as the end product. This is my favorite time to be in Liguria: the shadows lengthen, the air is crisp, but the sun is still shining. The crowds of summer tourists have dispelled, and the town is pleasantly quiet. The rest of the world feels very distant. Of course, it's easy to lose oneself in a bucolic fantasy when you're not actually trying to make a living off the land.

In fact, many young people are making the move back to the country, chasing an idyllic vision of an outdoor life, taking over agricultural family lands abandoned by the previous generation. Giada's grandfather, Dino Abbo, started the family business in the 1950s, and she has proudly picked up the torch. She is only twenty-four, with the fine, fragile features of a porcelain doll, yet none of the carefree exuberance of a twenty-year-old. After pursuing a high-paced marketing career in vibrant, metropolitan Milan, she made the abrupt decision to move back to her hometown and throw her skills into her family's business. She is serious, brow knit, when she speaks of the olive oil industry. "Ligurian oil should cost twice as much as it does, look at what we have to go through to cultivate and collect it," she gestures toward the steep hillsides, narrowly terraced with ancient dry rock walls, where only the tiniest and most daring of tractors will venture, if any. She is also referring to their unique *affiorato* olive oil, an extremely rare product made exclusively from the first drops of oil released with natural pressure, then painstakingly hand-decanted without the help of hydraulic presses or centrifuges.

"In the end, though, it's all worth it," she cracked the first smile of the day while gingerly wrapping a thin sheet of gold foil around a freshly filled bottle of bright green oil. "I get to finish what my grandfather started, to be part of that dream. I personally have a hand in every step of the production, from the tree to the bottle, to be sure it is the absolute best. I get to do something that represents my roots while looking toward my future."

Torta Pasqualina

Easter Artichoke Pie

For the crust:

2 recipes *Pasta Matta* (page 160)

Extra-virgin olive oil, for brushing

For the filling:

Juice of ½ lemon

10 small to medium of the most
   tender artichokes you can find

Extra-virgin olive oil

1 small white onion, halved
   and thinly sliced

Salt and pepper to taste

⅔ cup whole milk ricotta

¼ cup Greek yogurt

1 ½ ounces freshly grated Parmigiano-
   Reggiano (about ½ cup, packed)

1 teaspoon fresh marjoram

5 medium eggs (or 1 chicken egg plus
   10 quail eggs)

Makes one 9-inch tart

My mother-in-law, Fernanda, is famous for her *torta Pasqualina*, but rarely makes the dough from scratch anymore, opting instead for a store-bought puff pastry. However, as we spent the notorious Spring of 2020 on lockdown together in Moneglia, I cajoled her into teaching me the whole recipe from scratch. It was early on Easter morning; we were both still in pajamas. She rolled up the sleeves of her yellow bathrobe and dumped a pile of flour on the marble table in the kitchen, added some water, and began kneading. "My mother would roll the dough out with this, which I think was my grand-mother's," she said as she reached for a three-foot-long, time-worn wooden pin and began rolling. "And then she stretched the dough with her hands, until you could virtually see through it." Fernanda was straining her memory for the correct movements, as she tossed the dough over the backs of her hands. "In Genova, they say the Pasqualina should contain thirty-three layers of dough, one for each year of Christ's life, but nobody ever makes that many." After stacking about ten sheets underneath the filling, and seven on top, she showed me how to lift up a tiny corner of topmost layers and blow air into it, inflating the pie like a balloon. She quickly sealed the hole, trapping the air inside, before transferring the whole thing to the oven, resulting in a puffy, extra flaky, golden surface.

Besides the elaborately layered crust, this pie differs from other Ligurian torte because whole eggs are cracked into the filling; everyone at the Easter table hopes their slice contains one. My friend Valentina Venuti, who teaches cooking lessons at her *agriturismo* in Leivi, let me in on a little trick: She uses quail eggs in her *torta Pasqualina*. You can fit ten of the tiny eggs into the pie, which ensures every guest finds one in their slice.

Note: you can use frozen artichoke hearts instead of fresh to drastically cut down on the preparation time. Simply boil eighteen ounces of them in salted water until tender before proceeding with the recipe.

◆ Preheat oven to 350°F. Prepare the *pasta matta* according to instructions on page 160. Grease a 9-inch round baking dish or springform pan with olive oil; set aside.

Continued...

Fill a large bowl halfway full with cold water, add lemon juice. Cut off the top part of each artichoke, trim the stem, remove and discard tough outer leaves until you're only left with the softer lighter leaves closer to the center. Cut it in half and scoop out the hairy choke, if present. Cut each half into thin spears. As you work, transfer finished artichoke pieces to the lemon water to soak.

Heat 2 tablespoons olive oil in a large frying pan over medium-high heat. Add onion and cook, stirring occasionally, until translucent, 5 to 7 minutes. Drain artichokes and transfer to the pan. Add ¼ teaspoon salt and cook, stirring occasionally, until artichokes are tender, about 7 to 10 minutes. Transfer mixture to a large bowl and set aside to cool.

In a small bowl, stir together ricotta, yogurt, and ¼ teaspoon salt; set aside.

Stir Parmigiano into the artichoke mixture; add marjoram, more salt, and pepper to taste. Add 1 (chicken) egg and stir to combine.

Roll out a piece of the *pasta matta* as thinly as possible and begin layering it in the bottom of a prepared pan, according to instructions on page 160, brushing each layer with oil. I say the minimum is 4 layers underneath and 3 on top, though I usually opt for twice that many. As soon as the bottom layers are complete, scoop artichoke mixture into the pan. Spread the ricotta mixture in an even layer over artichokes. Create 4 egg-sized indentations in the filling (or 10 smaller ones if you're using quail eggs). Crack an egg into each hole and sprinkle each with salt and pepper.

Cover the pie with the top layers as explained on page 160, brushing the layers with oil. If desired, leave a small hole in the seam between the top and bottom layers of the pie at the edge of the pan after trimming away the excess, and blow into it, with the help of a straw, inflating the top of the pie like a balloon. Quickly seal the dough back together, trapping the air inside. Sprinkle the surface with a pinch of salt.

Bake the torta until golden and set, for 40 to 50 minutes. (If the surface browns too quickly, tent with aluminum foil.) Let cool for 1 hour before cutting and serving.

Pasta Matta per Torte

"Crazy" Dough for Savory Pies

The secret weapon of Ligurian *torte*, this simple, thin veil of a crust subtly encases the various fillings without overshadowing them. Depending on the desired effect, you can pile more or less of these thin sheets underneath or on top of your *torta*, brushing each layer with olive oil before adding the next. I often opt for two layers underneath the filling and three on top, but this recipe will provide you with enough dough for at least six layers. (You'll need to double the recipe if you're making the *Torta Pasqualina* on page 157.) The sheets should be paper-thin and translucent; roll the dough as thinly as possible with a rolling pin and then stretch with your hands until silky and sheer.

♦ Combine flour and water in the bowl of a stand mixer fitted with a dough hook. Knead on medium-low speed until a shaggy dough forms, about 5 minutes. Add olive oil and salt and continue kneading until dough is soft, smooth, and elastic, about another 7 minutes. Remove from mixer, form into a ball, and wrap tightly in plastic wrap. Let rest at room temperature for 30 minutes. Remove plastic wrap (do not discard) and cut the dough equally into 6 pieces. Cover the pieces with the plastic wrap to keep them from drying out, and let rest for another 10 minutes.

Preheat oven according to specific recipe instructions and lightly brush a 9-inch cake pan (preferably springform) with olive oil; set aside.

Place a piece of dough on a lightly floured work surface and roll into a disk with a flour-dusted rolling pin. Contrary to rolling out typical pie dough, you will want to roll out the edges first, rather than starting from the center of the disk, since the edges tend to shrink back as you roll. Begin rolling out the edges of the dough, turning the disk in a clockwise motion until it is large, round, and paper-thin. Dust your hands with flour, gently pick up the disk, and drape over the backs of your hands. Carefully stretch the dough, moving your hands away from each other and rotating the dough in order to stretch evenly. When dough is very thin and translucent, lay it over the cake pan. There should be plenty of overlap and it's okay if it doesn't sink to the bottom of the dish, as the filling will weigh it down later. Brush the sheet lightly with olive oil. Repeat the rolling and stretching process with one or two more pieces of dough, layering them on top of the sheet in the cake pan, brushing each sheet with olive oil.

Spoon desired filling on top of the sheets of dough. Lift up a small corner of dough to release any air that is trapped in the pan, then press it back into the pan and lay it over the edge.

2 cups (9 ounces) bread flour

½ cup room temperature water

2 tablespoons extra-virgin olive oil, plus more for brushing

½ teaspoon salt

Makes enough dough for one 9-inch tart

Repeat the rolling and stretching process with the remaining pieces of dough, laying them over the filling, and brushing each sheet with olive oil. After brushing the final layer with olive oil, gently press down on the edges of the pan, sealing the layers of dough together. Roll over the pan with your rolling pin, pressing firmly, in order to cut off excess dough and seal the edges. The bottom and top layers should stick together and fall away from the top of the pan, settling on top of the filling. Alternatively, you may trim away excess dough with kitchen shears, roll and crimp together the edges to form a decorative border.

Bake *torta* according to specific recipe instructions.

Torta di Cipolle

Onion Tart

One of my favorite *torte*, this classic Genovese tart combines sweet, stewed onions, creamy ricotta, and earthy porcini mushrooms for a savory vegetarian main.

1 batch *Pasta Matta* (recipe on opposite page)

2 pounds white onions, peeled and sliced

½ cup dried porcini mushrooms

2 tablespoons extra-virgin olive oil

3 tablespoons unsalted butter

¾ teaspoon salt, divided

3 ½ ounces freshly grated Parmigiano-Reggiano (about 1 cup, packed)

½ cup whole milk ricotta

1 large egg

¼ teaspoon freshly ground black pepper

Makes one 9-inch tart

♦ Preheat oven to 350°F. Prepare the *pasta matta* dough according to instructions on page 160. Grease a 9- or 10-inch round baking dish or springform pan with olive oil; set aside. While the dough is resting, place dried mushrooms in a small bowl, cover with hot water, and set aside to soak for 15 minutes.

Boil the sliced onions in a large pot of generously salted water for 2 minutes; drain thoroughly.

Drain mushrooms, squeeze to release excess water, and finely chop.

Heat olive oil and butter in a large frying pan over medium heat. Add onions and ¼ teaspoon salt and cook, stirring occasionally, for 5 minutes. Add diced mushrooms, lower heat to minimum, and continue cooking until onions are light golden and fragrant, 5 to 10 more minutes.

Transfer onion mixture to a large bowl and set aside to cool. When mixture has cooled, add Parmigiano, ricotta, egg, ½ teaspoon salt, and pepper; stir to combine.

Roll out the *pasta matta* as thinly as possible and layer it in the bottom of prepared pan according to instructions on page 160, brushing each layer with oil. As soon as the bottom layers are complete, scoop filling into the pan and spread evenly. Cover the pie with the top layers as explained on page 160, brushing each layer with oil. Bake until light golden and set, about 40 minutes. Let cool for at least 20 minutes before slicing and serving. Serve warm or at room temperature.

Torta Verde

Green Tart

Madamadorè in Imperia is famous amongst locals for its vegetable tarts and *sardenaira*, but I would never have discovered this unassuming little café without an insider tip. I fell in love with this tart through the glass display case before I even tasted it. Only about an inch high, a paper-thin, golden crust encases a dark green filling that smells vaguely of mountain pastures and freshly cut grass. This is a far cry from the eggy, cream- and bacon-filled, soggy disasters that passed for quiche during my childhood. I immediately poked my head into the cramped, hectic kitchen and asked for the recipe. If they hadn't told me, I wouldn't have even noticed the handful of cooked rice they throw into the filling to help bind it all together and lighten up the consistency of the greens. There are many different recipes for *torta verde* throughout Liguria: some contain much more rice or cheese, some call for sautéed onion or garlic. This, however, is my favorite version; I love how the simplicity of it accentuates the fresh flavor of the greens.

1 recipe *Pasta Matta* (see page 160)

2 ½ pounds Swiss chard or mixed greens (a mix of borage, beet tops, spinach, and escarole would be nice)

2 large eggs, lightly beaten

3 ½ ounces freshly grated Parmigiano-Reggiano (about 1 cup, packed)

½ cup cooked white rice, cooled

1 tablespoon minced fresh marjoram

½ teaspoon salt

Makes one 9-inch tart

♦ Preheat oven to 350°F. Prepare the *pasta matta* according to instructions on page 160. Grease a 9-inch round baking dish or springform pan with olive oil; set aside.

Wash the greens and boil in a large pot of generously salted water until tender, 2 to 3 minutes; drain. When cool enough to handle, wring out excess moisture with your hands, transfer to a cutting board, and finely chop; place in a large bowl. Add eggs, Parmigiano, rice, marjoram, and salt; stir to combine.

Roll out the *pasta matta* as thinly as possible and layer it in the bottom of prepared pan, and brushing each layer with oil, according to instructions on page 160. As soon as the bottom layers are complete, scoop filling into the pan and spread evenly. Cover the pie with the top layers as explained on page 160, brushing each layer with oil. Bake until light golden and cooked through, about 40 minutes. Let cool for at least 30 minutes before slicing and serving. Serve warm or at room temperature.

Torta di Zucca

Pumpkin Tart

This is another popular savory pie, though unfortunately not in my husband's family. I have tried my best to convert them to "team pumpkin," offering up countless soups, risottos, ravioli, and desserts starring my favorite orange vegetable, but it's hopeless. I assume they share traumatic childhood memories of the stuff and I have given up the battle. But if you share my affection for pumpkins, this tart is a fun addition to your repertoire. Feel free to substitute the pumpkin purée with roasted and blended butternut squash. This tart makes a lovely vegetarian main course, served warm or at room temperature. Pair it with a *Spinaci alla Genovese* (see page 148) and a cold glass of bianchetta (see page 215).

1 batch *Pasta Matta*
   (recipe on page 160)

1 tablespoon extra-virgin olive oil

1 leek, halved and thinly sliced, white and light green parts only

1 ½ cups (10 ½ ounces) pumpkin purée (canned or homemade)

½ teaspoon fresh thyme, minced

⅓ cup whole milk ricotta

½ teaspoon lemon juice

2 large eggs, lightly beaten

2 large egg yolks

1 ½ oz freshly grated Parmigiano-Reggiano (about ½ cup, packed)

½ teaspoon salt

Makes one 9-inch tart

◆ Preheat oven to 350°F. Prepare the *Pasta Matta* according to instructions on page 160. Grease a 9-inch round baking dish or springform pan with olive oil; set aside.

Heat olive oil in a medium frying pan over medium heat. Add leeks and a teaspoon of water; sauté until soft, about 5 minutes. Add pumpkin purée and thyme, stir to combine. Cook, stirring until all liquid has evaporated and the pumpkin mixture is shiny and fragrant, 3 to 5 minutes. Transfer the mixture to a bowl and set aside to cool.

In a small bowl, stir together ricotta and lemon juice; set aside.

Once the pumpkin mixture has cooled, add eggs, yolks, Parmigiano, salt, and ricotta mixture. Mix well.

Roll out the *Pasta Matta* as thinly as possible and layer it in the bottom of prepared pan, according to instructions on page 160, brushing each layer with oil. As soon as the bottom layers are complete, scoop filling into the pan and spread evenly. Cover the pie with the top layers as explained on page 160, brushing each layer with oil. Bake until light golden and set, about 40 minutes. Let cool for at least 30 minutes before slicing and serving. Serve warm or at room temperature.

Torta di Riso

Savory Rice Tart

Torta di riso has achieved such a cult status in Liguria that what was once merely a vehicle for yesterday's leftover rice is now a hotly contested recipe amongst home cooks. The wrong technique or proportions results in a spongy, dry, flavorless disappointment. Experts admit that the secret lies in a specific preparation of the rice (so much for recycling leftover risotto!); simmering it in milk before baking promises a soft, moist texture. After many experiments I have to agree, so that is the method I am providing here. This tart is so iconic of Liguria, there is even a famous comedy sketch entitled "*Torta di riso ... finita!*" ("*The rice tart ... is all gone!*"), which pokes fun at grumpy local hospitality, somewhat reminiscent of *Seinfeld*'s "Soup Nazi" bit. You may use a square or rectangular pan instead of the round one indicated here, but pay attention to the size: The finished tart should only be about 1-inch high.

♦ Preheat oven to 400°F. Prepare the *pasta matta* according to instructions on page 160. Grease a 10-inch round baking dish or springform pan with olive oil; set aside.

Combine rice, milk, and ½ teaspoon salt in a medium saucepan over medium-high heat. Bring to a boil, stirring occasionally, then lower heat to minimum and maintain a slow simmer. Cook, stirring occasionally, until rice is al dente, about 12 minutes. Pour rice and milk mixture into a bowl; the rice will continue to absorb the remaining milk as it cools.

In a small bowl, stir together ricotta and lemon juice; set aside.

Once the rice mixture has cooled slightly and absorbed the remaining milk, add egg, yolk, Parmigiano, nutmeg, ½ teaspoon salt, pepper, and ricotta mixture. Mix well.

Roll out the *pasta matta* as thinly as possible and layer 4 or 5 sheets of it in the bottom of prepared pan, according to instructions on page 160 , brushing each layer with oil. As soon as the bottom layers are complete, scoop rice filling into the pan and spread evenly. Trim the excess dough so you have about a 2-inch overhang on all sides, then fold it inwards to drape over the filling, leaving the center open-faced, and creating a decorative border. Brush surface of crust and filling with olive oil. Alternatively, you can cover the tart completely with more layers of filling, as instructed in the *pasta matta* recipe.

Bake until light golden and set, about 30 minutes. Let cool for at least 20 minutes before slicing and serving. Serve warm or at room temperature.

1 batch *Pasta Matta*
(recipe on page 160)
¾ cup uncooked arborio rice
4 cups whole milk
1 teaspoon salt, divided
¾ cup whole milk ricotta
½ teaspoon lemon juice
1 large egg, lightly beaten
1 large egg yolk
⅛ teaspoon nutmeg
1 ½ ounces freshly grated
Parmigiano-Reggiano
(about ½ cup, packed)
¼ teaspoon pepper

Makes one 10-inch tart

Forno

◆

Breads

In Italian, *il forno* translates literally to "the oven," but here, it refers to the many local bakeries that sell not only bread, pastries, focaccia, and slices of pizza, but also stuffed vegetables, savory tarts, quiches, and other baked goods. Historically, the *forno* had the importance of a communal hearth, as many locals didn't have ovens in the home. My mother-in-law recalls a parade of women carrying their unbaked savory pies and desserts, carefully packed in cloth bundles, to be baked in the *forno*'s oven on Sundays. They handed their goods over to the baker who cooked them, a few at a time, in the shop's oven. What followed was an unofficial ranking of the townswomen's cooking abilities.

"Did you see Simonetta's *torta di riso*? It's flawless."

"Flora's looks heavier than a brick."

"Ah, here comes young Adele, look at that *Pasqualina*! She will make a fine wife ... "

While it no longer serves as a communal oven, the *forno* is still the center of everyday life in Liguria. You smell the focaccia baking even before you join the eager mob crowded around the entrance. If you're lucky, a little machine at the door distributes paper numbers to bring order to the chaos, otherwise you will quickly be elbowed aside by petite, surprisingly strong, elderly women who know what they want and how to get it. When it's finally your turn, the server behind the counter is as impatient as you are, tongs in hand. "*Mi dica*," she barks. "Tell me."

If you make it this far, be sure to buy a sample of everything you see, but don't take too long or the *nonna* behind you in line will start shoving. The most important thing to order is the plain focaccia; it is the benchmark of the *forno*'s quality. If you make it out the door unscathed, act like a local and tear off a corner of your paper bag to shield your fingers from the oil as you break into a piece of hard-won, still-hot focaccia, while making your way back home through the *caruggi* (alleyways).

Ezio Rocchi, Sestri Levante

Focaccia

The first time I tasted real Ligurian focaccia (*fügassa* in local dialect) was my first day in Genoa and my first ever trip to Italy. After a whirlwind, three-week romance in Texas, I flew halfway across the world with my future husband to visit his hometown. Our first stop, naturally, was the neighborhood *forno*. The focaccia offerings enchanted me: olive-studded, sage-filled, or onion-topped, I wanted to try them all. Emilio ordered a sampling, and we sat on a green park bench in a nearby piazza to eat. I dove straight for the olive-topped version, but he stopped me, slipping a plain slice into my hands instead. "You must try the classic focaccia first. This is where everything begins."

If you've never been to the Italian Riviera and tried authentic Ligurian focaccia, it's hard to describe what you're missing. It's only an inch high, oily but not greasy, salty yet sweet, soft though not spongy. Even the topography is unique: crunchy, golden hills dive into soft, creamy valleys to create a delectable landscape, as pleasing to the eyes as it is to the palate. Here, focaccia is an institution, a birthright, a ritual. Contrary to most foods in Italy, it can be eaten any time of the day, even (gasp!) while walking down the street. Locals (myself included) dip a thin slice of focaccia in our cappuccinos in the morning, a custom that induces skepticism and disapproval amongst Italians outside this region.

To unravel the immensely complex world of *fügassa*, I contacted Ezio Rocchi, also known as "the king of focaccia," who comes from a long line of Genovese bakers. Amongst the precious gems of knowledge he bestowed upon me (many of which found their way into the following recipe), he let me in on a secret for eating focaccia: "If you watch closely, you'll notice the Genovese eat their slice upside down," he grinned, "that way, the tongue comes directly in contact with the salty upper surface, and the flavor is more intense."

I've included some variations and toppings on the following pages but you should really try your hand at the classic recipe first. After all, it's where everything begins.

Focaccia Ligure

Ligurian Focaccia

For the sponge:

¼ cup cool to lukewarm
(not hot) water

¼ teaspoon active dry yeast

1 cup (4 ½ ounces) bread flour

For the dough:

2 ¼ teaspoons active dry yeast

2 tablespoons lukewarm water

1 recipe sponge

3 ¾ cups (17 ounces) all-purpose
flour

1 tablespoon sugar

1 ½ teaspoons salt

1 cup plus 3 tablespoons cold
water, divided

2 ½ tablespoons extra-virgin
olive oil

For the pans:

Two 10 ½ × 15 ½-inch rimmed baking
sheets or jelly-roll pans
(alternatively, you may also use one
20 × 15-inch rimmed baking sheet)

¼ cup extra-virgin olive oil

For the brine:

1 cup hot water

1 ¾ teaspoon salt

To finish:

¼ cup extra-virgin olive oil,
plus more, for brushing

Makes two 10 ½ × 15 ½ -inch
sheets of focaccia

Start this recipe the night before to make the sponge starter, a yeast pre-ferment that provides the focaccia with a unique flavor and aroma. Don't be daunted by the lengthy instructions – the preparation is actually pretty straightforward. Be sure to use the best-quality, mild-tasting extra-virgin olive oil you can find; a bitter oil can ruin the entire batch.

♦ Prepare the sponge: The night before preparing the focaccia, stir together the water and yeast until the yeast dissolves. Add the flour and knead briefly by hand until a shaggy dough forms. Transfer to a small bowl or narrow jar where the sponge touches the sides yet has a little room to grow vertically (this is important in order for the sponge to develop correctly). Cover with plastic wrap and let sit at room temperature overnight (12 to 14 hours). Sponge should grow slightly and appear a little puffed up.

♦ Make the dough: The next day, dissolve yeast in 2 tablespoons of lukewarm water in a small bowl. In the bowl of a stand mixer fitted with a hook attachment, combine the sponge, flour, sugar, salt, and 1 cup plus 2 tablespoons cold water (you will add the remaining 1 tablespoon cold water later). Mix on low speed until a shaggy mass forms, about 2 minutes, then raise to medium speed and knead for about 5 minutes. Add the olive oil and the yeast-water mixture and continue to knead for another 5 minutes. Add the remaining 1 tablespoon of water and continue to knead until the dough is smooth and elastic, 5 to 10 more minutes. Cut the dough in half. Slightly stretch one portion of dough into an oblong shape, then fold into thirds, like folding a letter. Rotate the dough 90°, stretch, and fold into thirds again. Gently stretch the dough into a rounded brick shape and set aside on a lightly floured work surface, folded side down. Repeat with the other portion of dough. Dust the tops lightly with flour, cover with a clean kitchen towel or plastic wrap and let rest for 30 minutes.

♦ Prepare the pans: Pour 2 tablespoons of olive oil in the center of each baking sheet and spread with your fingers to grease the bottom of the sheets, leaving a 2-inch border around the edge ungreased. Gently roll out each dough with a flour-dusted rolling pin to a thickness of about ½ an inch, and transfer both doughs to the oiled sheets. (The dough will not fill up the entire sheets; it will cover only about ¾ of the surface area at this point.) Cover sheets with a clean dish towel or plastic wrap and let rise in a draft-free place for 20 to 25 minutes.

♦   Proof in pans: Uncover, dust lightly with flour, and gently stretch the dough to the ungreased edges of the pan. (If you pull a corner and it springs back, cover the dough and let it rest another 15 to 25 minutes until it holds its shape when stretched.) Press the dough into the edges of the pan with your fingertips, creating a seal so that the brine won't seep under later. Cover and set aside to rise for 1 hour to 1 hour and 15 minutes.

♦   For the brine: Stir together hot water and salt until the salt is completely dissolved, 3 to 5 minutes. Uncover the dough and test with your finger; if it springs back when you make a firm indentation in the dough, it's not ready yet. Cover and let proof a little longer until the indentation remains when firmly pressed. Sprinkle the surface with a bit of flour. Place one baking sheet on the table in front of you with the short side closest to you. Use only your index, middle, and ring finger at a 45° angle from the pan. You don't want to use only the tips as if you were typing on a keyboard, but the entire pad of your fingers as if you were trying to leave your entire fingerprint. Starting at the top, left-hand side of the tray, press the pads of your index, middle, and ring finger firmly into the dough, moving them very slightly forward and backward to elongate the dimples. Lift fingers and move down to create another 3 dimples about ½ an inch below the first row. Work your way down the entire left side of the pan, stopping a few inches from the bottom when the hand position gets uncomfortable. Repeat until the entire tray is dimpled, then turn tray 180° in order to dimple the remaining area. Repeat with the other tray of focaccia. Pour half of the brine over the dough in each tray and sprinkle each with 2 tablespoons of olive oil. The brine will seem like way too much but have faith! It should fill all the dimples. Let proof again for 40 to 45 minutes uncovered.

♦   Bake: Preheat the oven to 450°F with one rack placed in the upper third and one placed in the lower third of the oven. When the oven is hot, bake the focaccia for 15 to 18 minutes, rotating trays between the top and bottom racks and turning them back to front halfway through cooking time. The focaccia is ready when it is golden, but the dimples are still light beige. Remove from oven and brush immediately with olive oil. Remove from the baking sheet immediately and let cool upside down, so the bottoms don't get mushy. Eat warm.

Focaccia con la Salvia

Sage Focaccia

¼ cup fresh sage leaves

1 recipe *Focaccia Ligure* (page 174)

Makes two 10 ½ × 15 ½ -inch sheets
of focaccia

Use the freshest sage you can get your hands on for this recipe, and while you're at it, fry up any leftover leaves using the *Salvia Fritta* recipe on page 30.

◆ Gently wash and spin dry sage leaves and finely mince them. Add to the focaccia dough when you first begin kneading flour with the sponge and water. Continue preparing and baking the focaccia as instructed on page 174.

Focaccia con le Olive

Focaccia with Olives

While Taggiasche are the most famous local olives, you'll often find this focaccia studded with other, plumper varieties of black or green olives.

1 recipe *Focaccia Ligure* (page 174)

1 cup pitted olives
(Taggiasche, Kalamata, or other
pitted, plump, black or green olives)

◆ Prepare the focaccia recipe up until right after you dimple the dough with your fingers, but before you add the brine. Distribute the olives evenly over the focaccia dough, pressing gently to sink them into the dough, then add the brine and finish preparing and baking the focaccia as instructed on page 174.

Focaccia con le Cipolle

Focaccia with Onions

This is probably the most popular focaccia variety after the classic plain. Piles of thinly sliced onions add an irresistible sweetness when baked onto the surface of the dough. White onions are the most popular choice for focaccia, but red onions would make a delicious and colorful variation as well.

♦ Prepare the focaccia recipe up until right after you dimple the dough with your fingers, but before you add the brine. Cut the onions in half through the core and slice thinly. Spread slices on a wide tray and sprinkle with salt; set aside for 10 minutes.

Distribute the salted onion slices evenly over the focaccia dough, then add the brine and finish preparing and baking the focaccia as instructed on page 174.

1 recipe *Focaccia Ligure* (page 174)
2 large white onions
¼ teaspoon salt

Sardenaira

Tomato and Anchovy Focaccia

Whatever you do, don't call this pizza; in San Remo, an error of the sort will only earn you eye-rolls and insults. Western Ligurians are proud of this ancient recipe and fiercely claim it predates Neapolitan-style pizza by several centuries. Semantics aside, *sardenaira* is undoubtedly a delight for the senses: a soft focaccia base slathered in tomato purée and garnished with whole garlic cloves, salty anchovy filets, capers, and aromatic oregano. The name is derived from "sardine," which was once a key ingredient in the recipe but has been replaced by anchovies over the ages. If you plan on omitting the anchovies, make sure to add an extra sprinkling of salt to the topping before baking.

For the dough:

2 ½ teaspoons (1 package) active dry yeast

¾ cup plus 1 tablespoon lukewarm water, divided

3 cups (13 ½ ounces) all-purpose flour

1 teaspoon sugar

1 ¼ teaspoon salt

¼ cup extra-virgin olive oil, plus more for greasing bowl and pan

For the topping:

1 14-ounce can tomatoes, strained

¼ teaspoon salt

10 cloves garlic, unpeeled

¼ cup pitted Taggiasche olives

1 tablespoon capers, rinsed

10 to 12 oil-packed anchovy filets

½ teaspoon dried oregano, or more to taste

2 tablespoons extra-virgin olive oil

Makes one 10 ½ × 15 1½-inch tray of sardenaira

♦ In a small bowl, combine yeast with ¼ cup of the lukewarm water. In the bowl of a stand mixer with a dough hook attachment, combine the flour, sugar, salt, and remaining ½ cup plus 1 tablespoon water. Mix on low speed until a shaggy mass forms, about 3 minutes. Add the olive oil and the yeast-water mixture; continue to knead until the dough is smooth, elastic, and passes the windowpane test (see page 187), about 8 to 10 more minutes, starting on low speed and gradually increasing to medium speed. Transfer the dough to a large bowl lightly greased with olive oil. Cover with plastic wrap and set aside until doubled in size, about 1 hour.

Grease a 10 ½ -by-15 ½-inch jelly roll pan or a 11-by-17-inch rimmed baking sheet with 2 tablespoons of olive oil. When the dough is ready, remove it from the bowl and transfer it to the prepared baking sheet. Gently stretch and pat the dough until it reaches the edges of the pan (it might pull back a little in the corners: that's ok). Cover the pan with a clean kitchen towel and set aside for another 30 to 45 minutes, until it has risen a little and begins to spring back slightly when poked with a finger.

♦ For the topping: Set an oven rack in the lowest position, then preheat the oven to 415°F. In a small bowl, stir together strained tomatoes and salt. Spread the mixture evenly over the surface of the dough. Scatter unpeeled garlic cloves, olives, capers, and anchovies on top. Sprinkle with oregano and drizzle with 2 tablespoons of olive oil. Place the pan on a larger baking sheet in order to catch any oil or tomato sauce that bubbles over during baking, and transfer to the oven.

Bake the *sardenaira* on the lowest oven rack until golden on the edges and bubbling, 22 to 25 minutes. Transfer immediately to a cutting board and let rest at least 5 minutes before cutting into squares. Serve hot or at room temperature.

Farinata

Chickpea Flatbread

While it's often described as a "chickpea pancake" or "tart," neither of those terms adequately describes the texture and consistency of this popular and ancient Ligurian street food. When made correctly, it should be thinner than a pancake, with a crisp, flakey exterior and a soft, almost custardy center. Naturally vegan and gluten-free, the recipe appears deceptively simple thanks to its short ingredient list: water, chickpea flour, salt, and oil. Don't be fooled; the devil is in the details when it comes to making *farinata*. It's traditionally cooked in a piping-hot, wood-fired oven in wide, round copper pans, so adapting the recipe to a home kitchen required quite some tweaking. The exact proportions of water to flour are fundamental here, as is the long rest time and, most of all, the thickness of the batter in the pan, which should never exceed ¼ of an inch (6 millimeters). Therefore, it is not advised to double the recipe or use a different size pan than the one indicated here.

♦   Pour the chickpea flour into a large bowl and toss with a fork to loosen. Slowly add lukewarm water, a little at a time, whisking until smooth. Cover with plastic wrap and set aside to rest at room temperature for 6 to 8 hours. Every 2 hours stir the mixture and skim the surface to remove any foam that forms on top.

Place an oven rack in the lowest position and one in the highest position and preheat to 500°F. Place a rectangular 11-by-17-inch sheet pan or jelly roll pan on either rack in the oven while it preheats.

Meanwhile, heat olive oil in a small saucepan over medium-low heat. Do not let it come to a simmer; it should be hot but not smoking.

Remove the pan from the oven and let it cool until it is warm to the touch but not scalding. Add the salt to the *farinata* batter and stir to combine. Slowly pour the warm olive oil directly into the pan, swirling to coat. Pour the batter swiftly into the center of the pan. Bake on the bottom rack of oven for 20 minutes, or until *farinata* is light golden. If your oven permits, you may also bake it directly on the floor of the oven for this step.

Turn on the broiler to high and move the *farinata* to the top rack. Broil, watching closely, until a light brown crust forms on the surface, 2 to 4 minutes.

Remove from oven and let cool in pan for 5 minutes. Cut into 12 rectangles and serve hot.

2 cups (7 ounces) chickpea flour

2 ½ cups lukewarm water

1 ½ teaspoons salt

½ cup extra-virgin olive oil

Makes one 11 × 17-inch tray
   of farinata

Farinata con le Cipolle

Farinata with Onions

1 large yellow or red onion
¼ teaspoon salt
1 recipe Farinata (page 181)

Makes one 11-by-17-inch tray
of *farinata*

I love this variation on classic *farinata* that has sweet onions baked into the batter. While local *forni* most often use white or yellow onions, red onions stand out nicely against the golden-yellow backdrop. You may cut onions into strips or rings, just make sure they are very thin; use a mandolin if you have one.

♦   Peel onion and cut into paper-thin slices. Sprinkle slices with salt and set aside for 10 minutes. As soon as you pour the batter into the pan, sprinkle the onion slices evenly over the batter. Bake according to recipe instructions on page 181.

Gallette del Marinaio

Ligurian Sea Biscuits

4 cups (18 oz) all-purpose flour
Scant ½ teaspoon active dry yeast
1 teaspoon sugar
1 ½ cups lukewarm water
¼ teaspoon salt

Makes a dozen *gallette*

This ancient bread of Genovese sailors was born for lengthy sea voyages, being inexpensive, long-lasting, and soothing to seasick bellies. Most seafaring cultures have their own version of *gallette del marinaio*, also known as sea biscuits or hardtack. Often softened with seawater before using, these tough, dry, cracker-like biscuits are not intended to be eaten alone, but surface as a key ingredient in many Ligurian recipes, including *Cappon Magro* (page 117) and *Condiggiòn* (page 38).

♦   In the bowl of a stand mixer fitted with a dough hook attachment, combine the flour, yeast, sugar. Mix on low speed and slowly add water until a shaggy mass forms, about 5 minutes. Add the salt and continue to knead until the dough is smooth and elastic about 10 more minutes. Remove dough from bowl, cut in half, and form two balls. Place the balls on a lightly floured work surface. Cover loosely with plastic wrap or a clean kitchen towel and let rise until doubled in size, about 1 hour. Divide the dough into 12 equal pieces and roll each into a ball. Cover the balls with a clean kitchen towel and let rest for 30 minutes. On a lightly floured work surface, roll out each ball into a very thin, 4-inch disk. Transfer the disks to 2 parchment-lined baking sheets, spacing them at least 2 inches apart. Cover with a kitchen towel and set aside to rise for another hour.

Preheat oven to 400°F. Poke the surface of each *galletta* several times with a fork. Cook for 30 minutes or until golden. Let cool completely before using or storing.

Focaccia col Formaggio

Cheese Focaccia

The pride and joy of Recco, *focaccia col formaggio* is hardly focaccia at all, but equally as enchanting as its namesake. It is unleavened; two thin, crisp veils of dough encase a creamy, tangy cheese filling that oozes out when sliced. When in Recco, don't miss the opportunity to dine at one of the city's historic restaurants: Da Ö Vittorio and Manuelina. Named after the owner back in 1885, who is also credited with inventing the now-famous recipe, Manuelina is run by the fourth generation of the same family today. They passionately serve tray after bubbling tray of *focaccia col formaggio* to guests who travel from far and wide to sample their specialty.

While it's impossible to replicate the exact taste and consistency of Recco's *focaccia col formaggio* at home, the following recipe comes pretty close. The most difficult part will be getting your hands on crescenza or stracchino cheese, but there is really no appropriate substitute. If you have leftover dough, you could substitute it for *Pasta Matta* (recipe on page 160) in any of the *torta* recipes (pages 157 through 167).

4 ⅔ cups (21 ounces) bread flour

1 ½ cups lukewarm water

¼ cup extra-virgin olive oil, plus more for greasing pans and brushing

2 teaspoons salt

2 ¼ pounds crescenza or stracchino cheese

Makes two 11 × 17-inch trays of focaccia

◆ Combine flour and water in the bowl of a stand mixer fitted with a dough hook. Knead on medium-low speed until a shaggy dough forms, about 5 minutes. Add olive oil and salt and continue kneading until dough is soft, smooth, and elastic, about another 7 minutes. Remove from mixer, form a ball, and wrap tightly in plastic wrap. Let rest at room temperature for 30 minutes. Unwrap dough, cut into 4 equal-sized pieces, cover with a clean dish cloth, and let rest for 10 more minutes.

Preheat oven to 450°F and generously grease two 11-by-17-inch rimmed baking sheets with olive oil; set aside.

Continued...

Place a piece of dough on a lightly floured work surface and roll into a disk with a flour-dusted rolling pin. Contrary to rolling out typical pie dough, you will want to roll out the edges first, rather than starting from the center of the disk, since the edges tend to shrink back as you roll. Begin rolling out the edges of the dough, turning the disk in a clockwise motion until it is large, round, and thin. Dust your hands with flour, gently pick up the disk, and drape over the backs of closed fists. Carefully stretch the dough, moving your fists away from each other and rotating the dough in order to stretch evenly. When dough is very thin and translucent, lay it over one of the prepared pans; there should be plenty of overlap.

Distribute half of the cheese evenly over the sheet of dough in rounded, tablespoon-sized dollops; there is no need to spread it. Roll and stretch another sheet of dough, following the instructions above, then lay it over the baking sheet on top of the cheese. Press firmly around the edges of the pan with your hands to seal the two sheets of dough together. Set aside assembled focaccia to rest for 10 minutes. Meanwhile repeat this entire process to assemble another focaccia in the other pan, using remaining dough and cheese.

Cut excess dough from the edges of the first focaccia with a sharp knife. Alternatively, you can roll a large rolling pin over the pan, which will cut away the excess dough. Crimp the top and bottom layers together around the edges if they become unsealed. Using your thumb and forefinger, pinch the top layer of dough, ripping a quarter-sized hole in the sheet (you may also use a small knife if you prefer). Repeat this process, pinching about 10 holes around the surface of the focaccia; this will release the air trapped inside and let the cheese ooze out over the focaccia's surface. Brush the focaccia with olive oil, place directly on the lowest oven rack, and cook until it is golden brown and cheese is bubbling, 8 to 10 minutes. Repeat with second pan of focaccia.

Cut focaccia into large squares and serve hot.

Kizoa di Castelnuovo Magra

Sausage-filled Focaccia from Castelnuovo Magra

4 cups (18 ounces) all-purpose flour

3 teaspoons (1 ½ packages) active
dry yeast

1 teaspoon sugar

1 ¼ cup lukewarm water, plus 2
tablespoons

2 tablespoons extra-virgin olive oil,
plus more for brushing and greasing
pans

1 ½ teaspoons salt

1 pound Italian pork sausage, casings
removed

Makes one 10 × 15-inch tray
of kizoa

This rare, sausage-stuffed focaccia is the specialty of Castelnuovo Magra, a charming hilltop village near La Spezia. Surrounded on three sides by the border with Tuscany, this corner of Liguria is heavily influenced by Tuscan traditions and ingredients like pork, which appears infrequently in the rest of the region.

♦   In the bowl of a stand mixer fitted with a dough hook attachment, combine the flour, yeast, sugar, and 1 ¼ cup lukewarm water. Mix on low speed until a shaggy mass forms, about 5 minutes. Add the olive oil, salt, and remaining 2 tablespoons water; continue to knead until the dough is smooth and elastic, about 10 more minutes, starting on low speed and gradually increasing to medium speed until it passes the windowpane test (stretch a small piece of dough between your fingers into a thin translucent membrane. If the dough stretches without it breaking, it is ready to rise). Remove dough from bowl, cut in half, and form into two balls. Place the balls on a lightly floured work surface. Cover loosely with plastic wrap or a clean kitchen towel and let rise until doubled in size, about 30 minutes.

Lightly grease a 10-by-15-inch rimmed baking sheet or jelly roll pan. On a lightly floured work surface with a lightly floured rolling pin, roll one of the balls out into a rectangular shape and transfer it to the prepared pan, stretching and patting it to the edges. Break the sausage into small pieces and distribute it evenly over the dough in the pan; drizzle with 2 tablespoons olive oil. Roll out the other ball of dough and lay it over the sausage. Crimp together the edges of the top and bottom sheets to seal. Cover focaccia with a clean kitchen towel and set aside to rise for another 30 minutes.

Preheat oven to 415°F. Poke several holes in the top layer of the focaccia with a fork or sharp knife to let steam escape and brush with olive oil. Bake until golden brown and fragrant, 17 to 20 minutes.

Dolci

◆

Desserts

Genoa has a long, time-honored tradition of sweets. Initially influenced by early trade with the Far East, and later, by nineteenth-century French confectionary arts, compounded by the abundance of sugar in their ports, the Genovese cultivated a rich, refined pastry and candy culture. Nowhere is this more evident than in the antique confectionery and pastry shops of the city's vibrant historical center. Ornate and meticulously arranged shop windows peek in on hand-carved wooden cabinets, marble countertops, chandeliers, and frescos; mirrored walls are lined with elegant glass jars full of multicolored candies. Both Wes Anderson and Willy Wonka would approve.

Genovese are strict about the distinction between *confetterie* (confectionery shops), specializing in candies, syrups, chocolates, and other shelf-stable goods, and *pasticcerie* (pastry shops) with their cakes, cream puffs, and any other treats typically prepared in an oven. While there is some overlap in their offerings, the shops tend to identify devoutly with their classification.

Confectioner Pietro Romanengo has been serving the same, fiercely safeguarded recipes for more than two centuries. They expertly transform fruit, nuts, flowers, cocoa, sugar, and spices into candied fruits, *marrons glacés*, marzipan, chocolates, gelées, and hard candies. The historic shop, in Genoa's Soziglia district, is one of the city's gems and a must-see for any sweet-toothed traveler. A colorful sampling of Romanengo sweets, nestled in a decorative wooden box more appropriate for jewelry than candy, impeccably hand-wrapped in dark blue paper, and tied with white twine, is a fixture at our family's Christmas table. When we're in the market for pastries, cakes, or *pandolce*, however, we head to historic Pasticceria Profumo which also boasts nearly two hundred years of history in the city, and offers an equally enchanting, multi-sensory experience in the tiny downtown shop.

While many of these candies and chocolates are too complex (and top secret) to prepare at home, Liguria also has a long tradition of cakes, cookies, and other sweets prepared in home kitchens. This chapter explores some of these delightful desserts and offers you a taste of the region's rich (and sweet) history.

Torta Stroscia di Pietrabruna

Extra-virgin Olive Oil Shortbread Cake

2 ⅓ cups (10 ½ ounces)
 all-purpose flour, plus more
 for dusting
1 teaspoon baking powder
⅓ cup plus 4 tablespoons
 (4 ounces) sugar, divided
⅛ teaspoon salt
½ cup plus 2 tablespoons extra-virgin
 olive oil (preferably Taggiasca olive
 oil from Liguria), plus more for
 greasing pan
⅓ cup Marsala wine
2 tablespoons hazelnuts,
 coarsely chopped

Serves 8 to 10

This simple shortbread beautifully showcases the sweet, herbal flavor of Ligurian extra-virgin olive oil, also making it naturally vegan. It's no coincidence this cake hails from the village of Pietrabruna, immersed in the prolific, olive-producing hills of western Liguria. *Strosciare* in local dialect means "to break" because tradition dictates the cake must be broken into pieces, never sliced, when served. Make in a twelve-inch round pan for the traditional, very thin, almost cookie-like version, or in a nine-inch pan to obtain (my favorite) a one-inch-thick shortbread cake with a unique texture. Either version is delicious served with vanilla ice cream or gelato.

◆   Preheat the oven to 350°F; grease a 12- or 9-inch cake pan with olive oil and dust with flour. Sift together flour, baking powder, ⅓ cup plus 2 tablespoons sugar, and salt in a large bowl. Begin stirring in the oil, a little at a time, alternating with the Marsala. Mix with a wooden spoon until a shaggy dough forms. Turn out onto a clean work surface and knead by hand until the dough comes together in a smooth, shiny mass. Pat into a circle and transfer to the prepared pan; smooth the top with your hands until it comes to the edges of the pan. Sprinkle with chopped hazelnuts and 2 tablespoons sugar. Bake until cake is golden, 35 to 40 minutes. Let cool completely before breaking (not cutting!) the cake into pieces and serving.

Pesche Ripiene

Stuffed Peaches

By now, you need no reminder about the Ligurian obsession with stuffed foods; they have surfaced in every chapter of this book. So, what better way to end a summertime meal than with a sweet baked peach, stuffed with candied orange and Marsala-soaked amaretti cookies? I love to serve these hot out of the oven with gelato or whipped cream.

♦ Preheat the oven to 350°F; line a rimmed baking sheet with parchment paper; set aside. Peel and dice only 1 of the peaches; set aside. Hollow out the cavities of the remaining peach halves, widening them slightly so they can contain more filling; transfer peaches to prepared baking sheet; set aside.

Pour the Marsala into a shallow bowl. Quickly dip the amaretti cookies in the Marsala, then transfer to the bowl of a food processor with a metal blade. Add chopped peaches, almonds, and candied orange peel, and blend until smooth.

Spoon the mixture into the peach cavities, and smooth into dome shapes. Brush peaches and filling generously with melted butter and sprinkle with sugar. Place in the oven and cook until peaches are tender and golden brown, about 30 minutes. Serve hot or at room temperature.

5 ripe peaches, halved and pitted

1 tablespoon candied orange
peel, diced

½ cup Marsala wine

3 ½ ounces amaretti cookies

¼ cup (1 ½ ounces) blanched
almonds

2 tablespoons unsalted butter, melted

2 tablespoons sugar

Castagnaccio

Chestnut Cake

Naturally gluten-free, this dense, thin cake is popular everywhere that chestnuts grow in Italy, especially in Liguria and Tuscany. It's never cloyingly sweet, sometimes borders on savory, and the distinctive, almost gummy, texture is different from what you would expect from a typical cake. Chestnuts were a staple of farmers and country folk, only partially replaced as the main component of their diet by the arrival of the potato in the late 1500s. The original, "poor" *castagnaccio* contained only water and chestnut flour, but over time was embellished with pine nuts, walnuts, raisins, candied orange peel, herbs, and spices.

½ cup raisins

5 cups (17 ½ ounces) chestnut flour

⅛ teaspoon salt

½ cup sugar

4 cups cold water

2 tablespoons extra-virgin olive oil,
   plus more for brushing

½ teaspoon fennel seeds (optional)

1 cup pine nuts

Fresh, whole milk ricotta,
   for serving (optional)

Serves 8 to 10

◆ Preheat oven to 180°F; brush a 9-by-13-inch baking dish generously with olive oil; set aside.

Place raisins in a small bowl and cover with cold water. Let soak for 30 minutes, then drain and set aside. Meanwhile, sift chestnut flour into a large bowl; stir in salt and sugar. Slowly add water, a little at a time, stirring constantly with a whisk to avoid forming lumps. Stir in 2 tablespoons olive oil, fennel seeds, half of the raisins and half of the pine nuts. Pour batter into prepared pan and scatter remaining pine nuts and raisins decoratively over the surface. Bake until golden brown and small cracks appear on the surface, about 35 to 40 minutes. Let cool completely before serving. Dollop fresh ricotta on top of each slice right before serving, if desired.

Baci di Alassio

Alassio Kisses

By Italian standards, this is a relatively recent recipe. These sweet, chocolate-hazelnut sandwich cookies were invented around 1910 by Rinaldo Balzola, whose family went on to trademark the name "Baci di Alassio," and founded the now-famous Balzola pastry shop in (you guessed it) Alassio. I visited the colorful beach town and spotted *baci* in every bakery window, varying slightly in shape, size, and flavor. I dragged my husband to five different pastry shops, bought every cookie I saw, and shamelessly conducted a rigorous and delicious taste test, an activity I highly recommend for your next trip to the area. After many unsuccessful attempts at recreating the cookies, I turned to local pastry chef Daniele Tasso, who generously provided me with his foolproof recipe.

♦ Line 2 large baking sheets with parchment paper; set aside. Place hazelnuts in a food processor and pulse until finely ground into a powder. Add cocoa powder, sugar, and baking powder; pulse to combine. Add egg whites, salt, and honey; mix on low speed until well combined. Transfer the mixture to a pastry bag with a medium-wide fluted tip. Pipe about 40 quarter-sized kisses on prepared sheets. Set aside to air dry, undisturbed, until their shiny surfaces turn slightly opaque, about 30 minutes to 1 hour.

Preheat oven to 350°F. Bake cookies, 1 sheet at a time, in the middle rack of the oven for 8 to 10 minutes. Transfer to a wire rack to cool while cooking the second sheet. Let cookies cool completely at room temperature.

Meanwhile make the ganache: Place the chocolate in a medium heatproof bowl. Heat the cream in a small saucepan over medium heat. When it starts to simmer, pour over the chopped chocolate. Let it sit for a few minutes, then stir with a rubber spatula until you obtain a shiny ganache. Stir occasionally with a whisk until cool to the touch — ganache should be smooth and thick, but still spreadable. (Do not let it cool too much, or it will be hard to pipe.) Transfer ganache to a clean pastry bag with a medium fluted tip.

Pipe a bit of ganache on the flat bottom of one of the cookies and press the bottom of another cookie into the chocolate, creating a sandwich. Repeat with remaining cookies and ganache. Set aside at room temperature until set, at least 30 minutes, before serving.

2 cups (9 ½ oz) hazelnuts,
  lightly toasted and skinned

⅓ cup plus 1 tablespoon
  unsweetened cocoa powder

1 ¼ cup sugar

½ teaspoon baking powder

3 medium egg whites (3 ¼ oz)

⅛ teaspoon salt

1 tablespoon plus ½ teaspoon honey

3.5 ounces dark chocolate
  (70% cacao) finely chopped

⅓ cup heavy cream

Makes about 20 small sandwich
  cookies

Frittelle con Pinoli e Uvetta

Pine Nut and Raisin Fritters

These flavorful fritters are popular during *Carnevale*, the festive period preceding Lent celebrated with colorful parties, costumes, and extravagant, mostly fried foods. Also known as St. Joseph's fritters, these sweet, pine nut and raisin-studded puffs are often prepared on March 19 as well, for the feast day of St. Joseph, which is also Father's Day in Italy.

2 large eggs

½ cup lukewarm water

2 teaspoons active dry yeast

¼ cup sugar, plus more for sprinkling

⅛ teaspoon salt

1 teaspoon Marsala wine

2 cups (9 ounces) all-purpose flour

¼ cup raisins

¼ cup pine nuts

Vegetable or grapeseed oil,
  for frying

♦ Beat eggs in a large bowl, and add water, yeast, sugar, salt, and Marsala. Stir to combine. Add pine nuts and raisins, slowly sift in flour, and stir until smooth. Cover and set aside to rise in a warm, draft-free place for 1 hour.

Heat 2 inches of oil in a wide, deep skillet or Dutch oven over medium-high heat until a drop of batter sizzles immediately and floats to the top when it touches the oil. With two tiny spoons, (½ teaspoon) scoop small balls of dough into the hot oil (using one spoon to scoop the dough and the other spoon to drop the ball into the oil). Fry, turning occasionally with a spider, until the balls have puffed and are golden, 2 to 3 minutes. Transfer to a paper towel-lined plate, sprinkle with sugar to taste, and serve immediately.

Pandolce Genovese

Genoa's Christmas Cake

Pandolce is to Genoa what the now-famous *panettone* is to Milan. This compact, fruit- and nut-filled Christmas cake is obligatory in Liguria during the holiday season. Steeped in history, folklore, and tradition, *pandolce* is adorned with a sprig of bay leaves to symbolize Christmas, and brought to the table by the youngest family member. The oldest of the family cuts the first slice, which is wrapped in cloth and given to the first alms-seeker who passes by.

Legend credits the city's sixteenth century Doge, Andrea Doria, with challenging local pastry chefs to create a dessert representative of Genoa's wealth and grandeur, a competition that presumably resulted in the invention of *pandolce*, but it was more likely the creation of the city's under celebrated housewives.

At historic Pasticceria Profumo you'll find both the "tall" version of the cake, *pandolce alto*, painstakingly prepared with sourdough starter, and the "short" version, *pandolce basso*, made with baking powder. This recipe, inspired by Profumo's, is for the latter, which is infinitely easier to prepare at home, yet still includes all the ancient flavors and aromas of this legendary dessert.

Note: Orange flower water, a distillate made from bitter orange blossoms, has been produced in Liguria for centuries and shows up in many local sweets. Look for it online or in specialty food shops, or substitute with a half teaspoon finely grated orange zest.

2 ⅓ cup (10 ½ ounces) all-purpose flour, plus more for dusting

1 teaspoon baking powder

⅛ teaspoon salt

½ cup unsalted butter, at room temperature

½ cup granulated sugar

Seeds from ½ of a vanilla bean

1 large egg

¼ cup lukewarm milk

1 tablespoon orange flower water

⅓ cup (1 ½ ounces) pine nuts

¼ teaspoon fennel or anise seeds

½ cup finely chopped candied orange peel

1 ½ cups (8 ounces) raisins

Makes one 9-inch cake

♦ Preheat the oven to 350°F, line a baking sheet with parchment paper; set aside. In a medium bowl, sift together flour, baking powder, and salt; set aside.

In a large bowl, beat together butter, sugar, and vanilla until creamy. Add the egg and beat on high speed until fluffy. Slowly beat in milk and orange flower water until combined. Stir in pine nuts, fennel seeds, candied orange peel, and raisins.

Slowly add the flour mixture to the egg mixture and stir to combine, but do not overmix. The mixture will be dense, and you might need to use your hands to incorporate all the flour. Turn the dough out onto a lightly flour-dusted work surface. Shape the dough into a smooth ball and transfer to the prepared baking sheet. Press gently to flatten slightly. Score a large triangle shape on the surface of the dough (this traditionally represents the Holy Trinity). Cook until golden brown and a toothpick inserted in the middle of the cake comes out clean, 35 to 45 minutes. Let cool before serving.

Sciumette

Pistachio Cream Floating Islands

Similar to the French *Île flottante*, this charming dessert consists of a soft, billowy meringue island floating in a golden sea of pistachio-spiked custard. In local dialect, *sciumette* means "little foams," probably because the soft, moist meringues are reminiscent of sea foam. The recipe has been floating around Liguria for hundreds of years, particularly popular in Genoa during the festivities.

♦ Heat the milk in a large saucepan over medium-low heat. Add the lemon rind and bring to a simmer, stirring occasionally. Meanwhile, in a large bowl, beat egg whites and salt on low speed until frothy, raise to medium-high speed and beat until soft peaks form. Begin to add sugar, 1 tablespoon at a time, and beat until glossy, stiff peaks form. Slowly beat in cinnamon. With 2 soup spoons, carefully drop meringue mixture into the simmering milk, using one spoon to scoop the mixture into a mound and the other spoon to gently drop it into the milk. Cook until puffed and firm underneath, about 1 minute, and then carefully flip the meringue using 2 clean spoons. Cook for another minute, then transfer to a plate. Repeat with remaining egg whites, cooking 3 or 4 spoonfuls at a time. You may need to re-whip the egg whites occasionally if they start to deflate. Set aside cooked meringues.

Filter 3 ¼ cups of the hot milk with a fine mesh sieve into a clean saucepan and add ½ cup chopped pistachios. Bring to a simmer over low heat and cook, stirring often, until it smells like pistachios, 5 to 7 minutes. Filter milk again.

Combine egg yolks and sugar in a medium saucepan. Place over very low heat and whisk constantly while very slowly adding the pistachio-infused milk. Stir in salt. Cook over low heat, stirring constantly, until the custard thickens enough to coat the back of a spoon, about 8 minutes. If the mixture is lumpy you may filter it through a fine sieve.

Pour mixture into a stainless-steel bowl in an ice-water bath. Let cool until lukewarm, stirring occasionally, about 5 minutes.

Divide the pistachio cream between serving bowls, place 1 or 2 meringues on top, garnish with remaining chopped pistachios, sprinkle with cinnamon (if desired), and serve immediately.

For the meringue:

5 cups whole milk

1 (½-inch wide) strip of organic lemon rind

4 large egg whites, at room temperature (reserve the yolks for the custard)

¼ teaspoon salt

½ cup sugar

¼ teaspoon ground cinnamon

For the pistachio custard:

¾ cup chopped pistachios, divided

5 large egg yolks

¼ cup plus 1 tablespoon sugar

1 pinch of salt

Cinnamon, for garnish (optional)

Serves 4 to 6

Latte Fritto

Fried Milk

While this fried custard is undeniably sweet, I've never actually eaten it as a dessert. Instead, it is often served as a coveted component of *fritto misto*, a welcome sugary bite in the midst of a savory fried meal. The thin, golden, crunchy crust gives way to a luxurious, (though often scalding) cream filling; it's no wonder these bits are the first to disappear from the platter, and it's a shame it's so often relegated to a supporting role. Hot out of the fryer and sprinkled with sugar, these golden morsels make for a delectable, showstopping dessert, fully deserving of center stage.

◆　Line the bottom and sides of an 8-inch square pan with plastic wrap; set aside. In a medium bowl, whisk together 2 egg yolks and 1 tablespoon sugar; set aside.

Stir together flour and about ½ cup of the milk in a medium saucepan until smooth. Place over medium heat and slowly whisk in remaining milk and remaining ¼ cup sugar. Add vanilla, lemon zest, and salt; cook over medium heat, stirring often, until it just comes to a simmer. Remove from heat and, whisking constantly, slowly pour about ½ cup of the hot milk into the egg yolk mixture, about 1 tablespoon at a time. Slowly whisk in another ½ cup of the milk mixture, stirring constantly to avoid curdling the eggs. Pour the yolk mixture back into the saucepan, and cook over medium-high heat, whisking constantly, until it thickens into a velvety, pudding-like texture, and a spoon leaves a trail, 2 to 4 minutes.

Pour the mixture into the prepared pan, spreading evenly with a rubber spatula, and set aside to cool at room temperature for 30 minutes, then cover and transfer to the refrigerator for at least 4 hours, or overnight.

When ready to cook, heat about 2 inches of oil in a wide, deep skillet or wok. Whisk together 3 egg whites in a shallow bowl (reserve remaining yolk for another use); pour breadcrumbs into a dish. Remove pan from refrigerator and invert custard onto a cutting board. Remove plastic wrap and cut the mixture diagonally into bite-sized diamond shapes (it helps if you wipe down the knife between slices and wet the blade). Dip each piece in the egg whites, then coat with breadcrumbs. When the oil is hot enough that a breadcrumb sizzles immediately, fry the custard in batches, without crowding the skillet, until golden. Transfer to a paper towel-lined plate, sprinkle with sugar, and serve warm.

3 large eggs, separated

¼ cup plus 1 tablespoon sugar,
　plus more for sprinkling

½ cup (2 ¼ ounces) all-purpose flour

2 cups whole milk

Seeds from ½ of a vanilla bean

½ teaspoon finely grated lemon zest

⅛ teaspoon salt

Vegetable or grapeseed oil,
　for frying

1 cup plain breadcrumbs

Serves 4 to 6

Pinolata della Val d'Aveto

Pine Nut and Almond tart

Pine nuts, I'm sure you've noticed by now, are a staple of Ligurian cuisine, providing crunch and flavor (and non-animal protein) to countless recipes in this book. This delicious and pretty tart pairs them with a chewy almond filling and a buttery pastry crust. There is no need to toast the nuts beforehand, as they will get plenty of color while baked on the surface of the tart.

For the crust:

2 cups (9 ounces) all-purpose flour, plus more for dusting

⅛ teaspoon salt

½ cup sugar

½ cup cold unsalted butter, plus 1 tablespoon, melted, for brushing

1 large egg

For the filling:

1 cup (4 ½ ounces) blanched almonds, or 1 ⅓ cup almond flour

1 cup plus 2 tablespoons sugar, divided

4 large egg whites

¼ teaspoon salt

½ teaspoon almond extract

½ teaspoon finely grated lemon zest

To finish:

1 cup (4 ½ ounces) pine nuts

Powdered sugar, for sprinkling (optional)

Makes one 12-inch tart

♦ Combine flour, salt, and sugar in the bowl of a food processor fitted with a metal blade. Pulse to combine. Add butter and pulse briefly until a crumbly mixture forms. Add egg and pulse until combined into a smooth dough. Remove from food processor, wrap tightly in plastic wrap, and refrigerate for at least 1 hour, up to overnight.

Brush a light layer of melted butter on the bottom and sides a 12-inch tart pan.

Remove dough from refrigerator. Roll out to about ⅛-inch thick on a lightly floured work surface, then transfer to prepared tart pan. Press to adhere the dough to the bottom and sides of pan. Trim off excess and briefly knead scraps into a ball, then press into a disc and wrap in plastic wrap. Poke a few holes in the bottom of the dough with a fork; then transfer tart pan and leftover dough to the refrigerator while you prepare the filling.

Preheat oven to 350°F. Combine almonds and 2 tablespoons sugar in a blender or food processor and grind into a fine powder, set aside. If using almond flour, simply stir it together with 2 tablespoons sugar in a small bowl.

In a large bowl, beat egg whites and salt on low speed until frothy, then raise to medium-high speed and beat until soft peaks form. Begin to add sugar, a tablespoon at a time, and beat until glossy, stiff peaks form. Beat in almond extract and lemon zest. Slowly fold in ground almonds, being careful not to deflate the meringue. Scoop the mixture into the prepared tart shell and sprinkle evenly with pine nuts.

Roll out the remaining dough and cut into 6 ribbons, ¾-inch-wide each. Place them over the filling in a crosshatch pattern, pressing to adhere to the edge. Trim off excess. Transfer tart to the oven and bake until golden and cooked through, about 40 minutes. If the surface begins to darken before the filling is set, tent the tart with aluminum foil for remaining cooking time. Remove from oven and let cool completely in pan before slicing and serving. Sprinkle with powdered sugar, if desired.

Vino

♦

Wine

I Vini della Liguria

The Wines of Liguria

Winemaking in Liguria is not for wimps and, in some of the vineyards I've visited, could be considered downright heroic. Most of the region is besieged by rugged, mountainous terrain: poor, rocky soil dominated by steep hillsides that often fall directly into the sea. However, despite the hardships and inhospitable landscape, Ligurians have been producing wine since the Etruscan and Roman eras.

Over the centuries, the rocky slopes have been carved into terraces, reinforced by hand-stacked, dry rock walls. These steep inclines are often entirely inaccessible to machinery, and harvesting must be done by hand, basket after basket of hard-won grapes carried out on strong shoulders. Some vineyards are accessible only by boat. I visited the dizzying, mind-boggling vineyard of A Trincea, perched on a treacherous mountaintop in the farthest corner of Liguria, a stone's throw from the French border. Hundreds of rock walls line the painstakingly terraced slopes, and 35,000 grapevines thrive on the precipitous rows; I was stunned by the back-breaking landscape and humbled by the testament to the will of humans to make wine.

Paradoxically, Liguria's problematic terrain is also what makes its winemaking possible. The plunging hillsides protect seaside vineyards from cold northern winds and expose the grapes to the warm sea breeze and mild climate, resulting in unique and delicious wines.

Previous: Cà du Ferrà vineyard, Bonassola

I have been most impressed by the young winemakers I met on my travels. A new generation is taking over their ancestors' vineyards, transforming unremarkable family wines into new, unexpected products, experimenting with organic and natural winemaking techniques. Davide Zoppi, for instance, left his sleepy, seaside town of Bonassola to pursue a law degree and subsequent career in Milan. There he met his future husband, Giuseppe, a marketing-savvy manager of a multinational corporation. After ten years in the bustling city, they made the radical move back to Bonassola to take over Davide's family wine business, Cà du Ferrà.

"I'm sick of hearing about all the difficulties, this obsession locals have with the legend of hard work. I want my wines to be youthful and glamorous, to speak of the beauty of Liguria, not only of its struggles," he told me as we sipped a cold glass of *Luccicante*, Cà du Ferrà's vibrant, almost salty vermentino, on a hot August day in the hills above Bonassola.

Together, Davide and Giuseppe reinvented the business. They implemented organic, sustainable viticulture and natural winemaking techniques, launched a slick marketing campaign, resurrected abandoned vineyards in the area, and began cultivating ancient and rare grape varieties.

They are not alone. I also visited Gilda and Edoardo, the young brother and sister team behind Il Torchio, who produce natural wines in Castelnuovo Magra (which also happens to be the home of the *Kizoa*, on page 187, just another reason to visit). They, too, were on entirely different career paths when they heeded the call to take over their grandfather's vineyard and transform it into something fresh and new. "Wine is a living thing, it must change, just like you and I change," Gilda smiled, "it must evolve with the times."

Of course, innovation is not proprietary of the young. Piero Lugano of Bisson was in his sixties when he first began to age his wine under water. He produces his sparkling wine with the classic method, then lowers them onto the Mediterranean seabed in metal cages, where they age beneath the waves for thirteen to twenty-six months. He named the resulting, unique sparkling white wine *Abissi*, or "abyss."

Not surprisingly, Liguria is not one of Italy's most prolific wine regions; it's actually amongst the least productive. However, its wines are worth seeking out as they are delicious, charming, and pair beautifully with the recipes in this book. The most common local wine grape is vermentino, which flourishes in every corner of the Italian Riviera. It's not a particularly high maintenance plant and thrives on sun and sea air.

"The sun, the wind, and the untamable stone are the main characteristics of a deeply Ligurian wine," mused Davide Zoppi, swirling his glass and squinting into the sun, "and when you take a sip, you should sense the hillsides plunging into the sea, you should feel like you're jumping into the waves."

Some Ligurian wines to try:

White Wine

♦

Vermentino: This is the most common wine in Liguria. I spend my summers drinking Vermentino del Golfo del Tigullio, which is grown and produced in the area around our summer home in Moneglia, and also includes the famous wines of Portofino. Vermentino dei Colli di Luni is also wildly popular in the area. Persistent, fruity, and dry, Vermentino pairs well with appetizers, seafood, and nuts. Try serving it with *Pansoti con Salsa di Noci* (page 81) or *Fritto Misto* (page 129).

Pigato: The pigato grape grows almost exclusively in Ponente, the western part of Liguria, where I recommend trying a Pigato di Riviera Ligure di Ponente. Considered to be more refined and elegant than vermentino, this lightly fragrant wine has delicate notes of aromatic herbs and goes well with savory vegetable tarts, seafood dishes, and pesto.

Bianchetta Genovese: Produced in Val Polcevera, the valley and hills surrounding Genoa, this is the classic wine of the longshoremen and sailors who frequented the city's port. It is a simple, straightforward, and extremely drinkable white whose famous pairing is, naturally, a crisp slice of Genovese focaccia. It also makes a great aperitivo with a steaming plate of *Frisceu* (page 33)

Colline di Levanto Bianco: This delightful white is produced in the province of La Spezia between Levanto, Bonassola, and Framura. Native grape varieties, bosco and albarola are blended with vermentino to create a dry, slightly briny, well balanced wine that pairs beautifully with vegetarian dishes like *Ripieni di Verdura* (page 145), and seafood like *Zuppa di Muscoli* (page 108), *Totani ripiene* (page 101) or *Acciughe Marinate* (page 46).

Cinque Terre Bianco: Bosco, albarola, and vermentino grapes make up this delicate, straw-colored white that has a hint of flowers and meadow herbs and produced inside the National Park of Cinque Terre. It goes nicely with light appetizers and seafood dishes.

Colli di Luni Bianco: Made from vermentino, trebbiano, and toscano grapes, this wine is delicate and harmonious, with floral notes and pleasant salinity. Pair it with soups like *Minestrone alla Genovese* (page 90), fresh salads like *Condiggiòn* (page 38), and seafood stews like *Stoccafisso accomodato* (page 114).

Red Wine

♦

Rossese di Dolceacqua: Made exclusively with the rossese grape, this flavorful, full-bodied red pairs well with rabbit, meat, and mushroom dishes and was a favorite of both Napoleon and Pope Paul III. Try serving it with *Coniglio alla Ligure* (page 125).

Ormeasco di Pornassio: The ormeasco grape was imported to Liguria from Piedmont around the 1300s and belongs to the same family as dolcetto. It has a ruby red color, dry, warm flavor, and notes of ripe red fruit, and pairs nicely with meat ravioli and *Tomaxèlle* (page 133).

Colli di Luni Rosso: This wine reflects its geographical proximity to Tuscany and is made with a blend of sangiovese (Tuscany's principal red wine grape) and Ligurian ciliegiolo. This ruby-colored, fragrant, light, and balanced red goes beautifully with ravioli and meat dishes.

Dessert Wine

◆

Cinque Terre Sciacchetrà: Pronounced "shah-keh-trah," this sweet raisin wine is as fun to say as it is to drink. Sciacchetrà is one of the most famous and exquisite wines of Liguria and is also under the protection of Slow Food. Made from bosco, albarola, and vermentino grapes, that are left to dry naturally for two months on racks, then crushed, the wine is then aged in small oak barrels for one year. The fresh notes of dried fruit and aromatic herbs pair well with aged cheeses, *Pandolce Genovese* (page 201), and *Pinolata della Val d'Aveto* (page 206).

Vineyards at A Trincea, Airole

Ringraziamenti
Acknowledgments

This project, like all books, was a team effort and couldn't have happened without the help and support of many wonderful people. Grazie, my entire Italian family and our cherished nonnas who welcomed me so completely into their beautiful lives. I am also eternally grateful to my Texan family who raised me to fearlessly love life and to see beauty everywhere.

Caitlin Leffel, meticulous editor and eternal optimist, thank you for smilingly keeping us on track in spite of a global pandemic and all the pitfalls that came with it. Laura Lazzaroni, my dear friend and mentor, this book wouldn't have happened without your constant support and sage advice. Thanks to Rizzoli for believing in this project, and to the strong visual team that made it beautiful: Gabriella Voyias and Charlotte Hauser on graphic design and Cecilia Carmana on prop styling. I'm grateful to Anna Kovel for her precise recipe editing and Erin Murray for the diligent testing. Thank you, Elizabeth Thacker Jones, for encouraging this book into existence and cheering me on every step of the way. Grazie, Gianluca Biscalchin for bringing Liguria to life with your illustration

The magnanimous Enrica Monzani generously shared countless secrets, tips, recipes, and stories of her beloved Liguria with me. Special thanks to Giuseppe Avanzino, for loaning me your advice, cookbooks, and knowledge of Ligurian dialect. Grazie to all the Ligurian people who opened their doors, hearts, and kitchens to me: the Pagliettini family, Enrico and Nadia of Cantine Cattaneo, Paolo Cagnoli, Ezio Rocchi, Valentina Venuti, Paolo Calcagno, Vladimiro Poma, Paola Allegra, Lorenzo of Trattoria Raieü, Gastronomia Quaini, Roberto Perrone, Emanuela Carbone, Pasticceria Confetteria Profumo, Daniele Tasso, Lavanda Riviera dei Fiori, Giada of Dinoabbo, Confetteria Pietro Romanengo, Davide Zoppi of Cà du Ferrà, Gilda Musetti of Il Torchio, and Laura Masala of A Trincea. Thank you Jill Mason, for the fresh eyes and last-minute copy edits.

Last but not least, thank you Emilio, my tireless photographer, my partner in crime, the love of my life. You brought me to this strange and beautiful land, you've followed my every whim and made all my dreams come true since 2002. Thank you for this life we've made together. Every day is an adventure with you.

First published in the United States of America
in 2021 by
Rizzoli International Publications, Inc.
300 Park Avenue South
New York, NY 10010
www.rizzoliusa.com

Copyright © 2021 Laurel Evans
Photography by Emilio Scoti

Recipe Consultant: Enrica Monzani
Stylist: Cecilia Carmana
Illustration on pages 16-17: Gianluca Biscalchin

Design: Gabriella Voyias & Charlotte Hauser

Publisher: Charles Miers
Editor: Caitlin Leffel
Production Manager: Colin Hough Trapp

Printed in China
Library of Congress Control Number: 2021935742

2021 2022 2023 2024 / 10 9 8 7 6 5 4 3 2 1

ISBN: 978-0-8478-7061-5

Visit us online:
Facebook.com/RizzoliNewYork
Twitter: @Rizzoli_Books
Instagram.com/RizzoliBooks
Pinterest.com/RizzoliBooks
Youtube.com/user/RizzoliNY
Issuu.com/Rizzoli